UNLIMITED

POTENTIAL:

How to Live When You're Called to More

Sven Lepschy

Unless otherwise indicated, all Scripture quotations are taken from the Holy Bible, New International Version®, NIV®. Copyright © 1973, 1978, 1984, 2011 by Biblica, Inc.™ Used by permission of Zondervan. All rights reserved worldwide. www.zondervan.com The "NIV" and "New International Version" are trademarks registered in the United States Patent and Trademark Office by Biblica, Inc.™

Scripture quotations marked (ESV) are from the ESV® Bible (The Holy Bible, English Standard Version®), copyright © 2001 by Crossway, a publishing ministry of Good News Publishers. Used by permission. All rights reserved.

Scripture quotations marked (NLT) are taken from the Holy Bible, New Living Translation, copyright ©1996, 2004, 2015 by Tyndale House Foundation. Used by permission of Tyndale House Publishers, a Division of Tyndale House Ministries, Carol Stream, Illinois 60188. All rights reserved.

Scripture quotations marked (TPT) are from The Passion Translation®. Copyright © 2017, 2018 by Passion & Fire Ministries, Inc. Used by permission. All rights reserved. www.thePassionTranslation.com.

Cover design: Virtually Possible Designs

Editing: writebylisa@gmail.com

ISBN 13 TP: 978-1-6631-0013-9

CONTENTS

SPECIAL THANKS

A very special thanks to my wife, Nathalie. Without her support and patience, I would not have been able to dedicate my time and energy toward writing my first book. Thank you so much for being my best friend and soulmate!

Thank you, Kevin and Kathi. You gave me the gentle push I needed and encouraged me to share my American dream. I thank God for connecting us and making me part of your ministry.

Thank you to my parents. I dedicate this book to them. Without them, I would not be where I am now. They invested precious time and money into me and always had my best interests at heart. They provided me with safety, security, and an upbringing with solid principles and values. They taught me right from wrong, and most importantly, they have given me love. I can't tell you how blessed I am to have parents like this. So many times, we take for granted our ability to rely on our parents and call and talk to them whenever we want. With that said, thank you, Mom and Dad, for all you have done for me. I will always be grateful. I love you forever!

FOREWORD

Kathi and I are very excited to introduce you to Sven Lepschy. Sven and his wife Nathalie have been a constant support to us personally as well as to Warrior Notes Ministries. Sven's new book, *Unlimited Potential: How to Live When You Are Called to More*, is his detailed story of how he, an immigrant to America, pursued and reached his potential. He desires is to add value to people through the avenue of aviation. Sven has already done this for me personally. Not only is he a great friend, but he is also one of my flight instructors in the Embraer Phenom 300E jet aircraft that we currently fly. Sven states in his new book, "Becoming your best and unlocking your unlimited potential lies in part with attitude and strategy. Your attitude comes from within you, which is up to you to change. What I can do to help you is share my own story of learning to unlock your potential."

Kathi and I believe God has a plan for every individual on earth. Psalm 139:16 states, "You saw who you created me to be before I became me! Before I'd ever seen the light of day, the number of days you planned for me were already recorded in your book" (TPT). I know that Sven's book will encourage you to follow God's special plan for your life. Don't let a setback discourage you from attaining your *Unlimited Potential!* One of Sven's favorite sayings is, "Yesterday ended last night. It doesn't matter if it was good or bad; it's done, over and past." Let go of the hurt of the past and let God perform a miracle in your life *today*. Enjoy this awesome book!

Dr. Kevin and Kathi Zadai
Founder and President of Warrior Notes and Warrior Notes
School of Ministries

PREFACE

Why did I write this book? Aviation is my passion, and my obsession is to add value to people. I have always made it a point to pursue my potential. I know I might never become the best in the world, but I know I can become my personal best. That is what drove me to write this book. Becoming your best and unlocking your unlimited potential lies in part with attitude and strategy. Your attitude, which is up to you to change, comes from within you. I can help you by sharing my own story of learning to unlock my potential. One of my favorite sayings is, "Yesterday ended last night." It doesn't matter if it was good or bad; it's done, over and past.

I don't want you to get stuck in the past because you can't change it. Don't let the past rule your future. When I meet new people and tell them where I came from, what I have managed to accomplish, and where I want to go in life, people always tell me, "Wow, what an incredible story. This is simply amazing!" I often think, *Why is it so amazing? I'm just a regular guy, and this is what happened to me.* I tell people, "You are in the same shoes as me. You can do what I have been doing, probably even faster than me."

Looking back, my life has been an incredible journey. I have been blessed with health, great friends, and open doors, all at the right time. When I reached those right doors at the right time, I also had the courage to walk through each door without knowing what was on the other side. I had to leave behind the room I was in and trust God to get to the other side. See, we are all afraid of going into a new place—the unknown. You cannot grow if you stay in your comfort zone. The only way to grow in life is to leave your comfort zone and get completely uncomfortable. Uncomfortable means that I do something I've never done before and might have never dreamed of doing before.

The first time I spoke to a large crowd, more than one hundred people were in the audience. I was introducing a new product that I wanted to demonstrate to the marketplace. I never thought I would be able to get a single word out in front of all these people looking at me and at a product I was trying to sell. Let me tell you, it was so scary being unsure of what to say and standing in front of a bunch of strangers as they watched me.

I know now the scary feeling is actually excitement. Once you move out of your comfort zone and feel comfortable outside it, it's exciting. If you stay within your comfort zone, it stays scary. It's like writing this book. I began by writing one word and then another word and then another. The key is to start; most people miss this very important part— starting.

I decided to write down my story and share it with you and the whole world. I want to give you hope, inspiration, and especially courage. I want to help get you out of your nine-to-five rut. I want you to create your own business and add value to other people rather than just exchanging time for money at your job. Two days before I started writing this book, my friend Kathi told me, "Sven, you ought to write a book!"

I told her that I always wanted to write about and share about my past and how my life has been filled with blessings. It's not hard to change your life and escape the daily rat race. Here we are now, and I am excited to take you on my journey. I truly hope you enjoy it as much as I have enjoyed opening my heart and writing my story for you.

1 | THE STORY

*Always focus on the front windshield
and not the rearview mirror.*
—Colin Powell

*If you talk about it, it's a dream, if you envision it,
it's possible, but if you schedule it, it's real.*
—Tony Robbins

*Ownership is not a vice, not something to be ashamed of, but
rather a commitment, and an instrument
by which the general good can be served.*
— Vaclav Havel

I was born in Frankfurt, Germany, in 1972. I grew up as an only child in a middle-class family. I know what you must be thinking. An only child. He was spoiled. Yes, you're right. I was spoiled but not with money or monetary things; I was spoiled with love from my parents. They gave me unlimited love, dedication, and attention.

As a young child, I loved money. I held paper money in my hand and put it in a little metal lockbox that my dad bought for me. It made me feel like a bank. I loved going to the bank, looking at the bulletproof glass windows, and seeing all the people working with the money that came in and out of the bank every day. Even as a small child,

As a small child, something in me realized that saving money was good and pleasurable.

something in me realized that saving money was good and pleasurable. My dad took me to the bank when he deposited money after work and got a receipt.

I had a wonderful childhood growing up in Germany. It was a safe country with a thriving economy; you could buy and eat whatever you wanted. The education system was excellent. And let's face it, Germany makes the best cars in the world. There are many good things in Germany; however, there are also many bad things there. I will explain later why I left Germany in 1994 for the great country I live in now, the United States of America.

My first language was Dutch; my parents only spoke Dutch to me for the first four years of my life. My mom was born in Indonesia, a Dutch colony, so she decided to teach me to speak Dutch before I started school. When I went to kindergarten, I finally learned how to speak German. As a child, your brain is like a sponge and can absorb so many different languages simultaneously; it's simply amazing.

You don't even realize how capable your brain is when you are young. You can easily take in information, store it, and process it. Even now, when I go back to the Netherlands or meet Dutch people here in the US, I notice that once I start speaking Dutch with them, it only takes about five to ten minutes, and I go from broken Dutch to having a fluent conversation with them.

While growing up at my parents' apartment in Frankfurt, my mom's sister, Hetty, was the primary person raising me for the first years of my life. I call her my second mom. In the 1970s, both of my parents worked, which was our family's norm. In other households at that time, the wife usually stayed home, managed the house, cooked meals, took care of the children, and cared for the family. However, this was not the case in our family. My parents were workers; they were not wealthy individuals and had to earn their money as they went. My dad was a sales manager with a British company, selling cast iron connectors for industrial companies. My mom worked in the accounting department for Qantas Airways, which explains my love of numbers, excitement in sales, and of course, my passion for aviation.

On my first day of work at my first job at a department store, my manager told me that we had an excess inventory of a particular calculator. He asked me to focus on selling only those models, although they were not the best when compared with other models. At the end of the day, my manager's jaw dropped when he looked inside the storage cabinet where all the calculators were stored. He asked me what I did with all the calculators. I answered, "I sold them all. Didn't you tell me to sell this specific model?"

After that, I was moved to the TV department. The commission was much higher for selling big-ticket items. I watched my colleagues and learned what to say to a customer when selling a TV. I asked many questions about which TV was the best quality with the least returns. I wanted to sell the best units to the customers so when they come back to the store, they would remember me and say, "That was a great TV you sold me. We are very happy with it. Thank you so much." I also checked the storage room to see what kind of supply we had. I always sold readily available units that I did not have to special order. My motto was "let's move product."

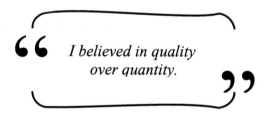

" I believed in quality over quantity. "

"Take delight in the Lord, and he will give you the desires of your heart" (Psalm 37:4 NLT).

At sixteen years old, I realized what people wanted, and when I gave them what they wanted, they were happy and always came back to buy other things. I believed in quality over quantity. I was amazed by the differences in products we sold. The place I worked had many high-end customers. I did not have a lot of resources to buy nice items, and if I wanted something, I had to save up for it. I was happy selling fewer items of higher quality as opposed to selling more items with lesser quality. I used to look at magazines with luxury items, such as watches, cars, boats, big houses, airplanes, and nice designer clothes. I daydreamed and visualized what I liked. My teachers in school always told me that I daydreamed too much; that's probably why I wasn't good at school because I didn't focus on what we learned, but I focused more on what I envisioned.

You can begin to dream about something you want by daydreaming and visualizing. First, you envision what you can get, and then one day, you can purchase it. I once went to an expensive German car dealer and sat in a German luxury car, smelling the new leather and caressing the stitching on the seats. What quality and craftsmanship! Visualizing is the first step, but experiencing the item you want will increase the odds of getting it. You have to see it, smell it, touch it, and feel it.

Since my mom worked for an airline, we could take advantage of staff travel benefits. This meant that we could travel practically for free around the whole world. My parents and I took full advantage of that benefit and flew to places others could only dream of: Asia; Australia; and the Pacific Islands, such as Tahiti, Fiji, and Hawaii. We visited North America, Canada, and countries in Europe. My favorite place to visit during summer vacation was California. My cousins lived there, and I couldn't wait to go back and visit them. I loved the houses, the cars, the open spaces, and nature. I loved the fast-food restaurants, the cities, the roads, and the big tall buildings. Once, we drove from California to Las Vegas. I was so amazed by the desert and how people could live in a city with nothing around them but sand. All the lights, twenty-four-hour businesses, casinos, and restaurants—it was heaven for me. There was nothing like it when I was growing up in Germany.

We went to New York, Chicago, Denver, San Francisco, Los Angeles, and Dallas. I learned a lot about American culture as a young kid. One afternoon, when I was in the backyard of my uncle's house in California, I envisioned myself holding a little blue booklet in my hand that said "Passport: United States of America." I was convinced that I would be living in this great country one day. I wanted it so badly that I envisioned it more and more each day. One of my biggest dreams came true the day I became a US citizen.

When you begin traveling around and meeting new people from different cultures, you appreciate how you grew up and were raised. You look at situations differently and see the world and people from a different perspective. You have heard this truism many times: "The grass is always greener on the other side of the fence." But let me tell you something—the grass here in the United States is the best in the world!

> *You look at situations differently and see the world and people from a different perspective.*

I was not the smartest kid in school, and I didn't like attending middle or high school. Year after year, I got by with passing and average grades. I wasn't the best, but I wasn't the worst either. My schooling took a turn when I had to repeat the ninth grade. I was held back because some of my grades were below average, and I failed a few classes. It was one more year of the same subjects, just different teachers. Guess what? Nothing changed a bit. I had the same failing grades and had to leave to attend a different school with lower standards. I made new friends there and felt much more comfortable with the teachers and the environment. I did not have to repeat any subjects; instead, I made above-average grades and finished at the top of the class. I was elected as a substitute class speaker. That was a big deal back then, especially because I was such an introvert.

During my childhood and into young adulthood, I developed a passion for aviation after being exposed to the airlines throughout my childhood. My mom managed to get me a week-long apprenticeship with her airline when I was in high school, which confirmed my passion. When I graduated at the top of my class, I was able to get a spot in a three-year program as an airplane mechanic for Lufthansa, a major German airline in Frankfurt. They offered this apprentice program for individuals who had finished high school and wanted to work in aviation maintenance. Alongside the apprenticeship, they offered a position in a technical school.

Our training in the program included time in a flight simulator. This was exciting because I had desired to learn how to fly an airplane for a long time. On one occasion, we went into the simulator to practice engine start procedures and taxiing the aircraft. We completed the four-hour training session in only thirty minutes, so of course, we spent the remaining three and a half hours practicing takeoffs, landings, and flying around the airport. It was the most fun I had ever had. Right then, I made up my mind that I would become a pilot. It confirmed my desire and passion for flying airplanes. After that, I applied as an airline pilot cadet with Lufthansa's flight school. After a three-year program, I graduated as an airplane and power plant mechanic and could work on Airbus, Boeing, and McDonald Douglas models.

In June 1994, my journey took me to Saint Augustine, Florida. I selected a flight school with many international students, mainly from Europe. Björn, the flight school manager, was European as well, so I felt comfortable there. When people are abroad, they look for a connection that makes them comfortable and reminds them of home. I started as a student pilot flying Cessna 152s, and after only three weeks, I passed and received my private pilot license. With forty hours of piloting time, I continued my instrument rating, which would allow me to fly using only the instruments in the cockpit as a reference.

Additionally, I pursued my commercial pilot's license, allowing me to work for a company, and my multi-engine rating, which enabled me to fly two-engine airplanes. After only seventy-two days, I completed 190 hours of flight time, three check rides with the Federal Aviation Administration (FAA), three written exams, and my commercial pilot check ride. With this qualification, I could fly commercially for a business or airline. However, I had very few flight hours compared to all the other pilots applying for jobs.

In the meantime, I accumulated additional flying hours and started converting my European airplane mechanic license to an FAA airframe and power plant (A&P) certificate. I had to take three written exams, an oral exam, and a practical exam. Within a month, I had my US mechanic's license, based on my three years of experience with Lufthansa. I was looking for jobs left and right, but since I did not have a work permit or a Green Card, and I could not get a job here in the United States.

I reached out to my cousin in Indonesia, who was working for a small commuter airline there. He told me that the airlines were looking for co-pilots. So my next stop on the journey was Indonesia. After arriving there, I stayed with my cousin at his little apartment. I could not wait to meet the chief pilot of his airline and interview for a pilot position.

He arranged an interview for me and accompanied me to the chief pilot's office. The chief pilot seemed satisfied with my experience and documentation and only required that I obtain an Indonesian-issued medical certificate. Everything seemed to be on track, and I was going through the process of having my US medical certificate transferred to Indonesia. Then, my mom called. She informed me that she received a certified letter from the German military with my draft papers—one-year mandatory service in the German military. I explained that I would not be returning to Germany because I had a job lined up.

Not responding to a mandatory draft would put me at risk of jail if I returned to Germany. My mom was very angry when I told her I would not be returning. Right after I hung up, my dad called. Of course, he convinced me to come back and do my military service; after all, it was only one year. On my way back to Germany, I had already begun looking for flying jobs near my hometown of Frankfurt. My ultimate goal was to continue flying.

I inquired about becoming a pilot with the German Air Force. They explained that required a twelve-year commitment to join the German Air Force and become a fighter pilot. Oh well! I gladly declined and only committed to my twelve-month mandatory service, which was three months of boot camp, followed by nine months of office work. I was lucky because I was stationed very close to my hometown and worked only during night shifts for twelve hours. That meant I had a four-day week. In the meantime, I flew small airplanes and collected flight time, which made me more attractive to commuter airlines. As a newly qualified pilot, you don't get hired at a major airline right away. Instead, you start with a small airline and work your way up.

"The heart of a man plans his way, but the Lord established his steps" (Proverbs 16:9 ESV).

During my military service, I applied for the Green Card lottery. The US government had started a program called the

Diversity Immigrant Visa Program. Back then, all you had to do was send in a piece of paper with your first name, last

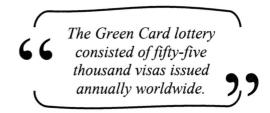

> *The Green Card lottery consisted of fifty-five thousand visas issued annually worldwide.*

name, date of birth, current address, and country of citizenship. The only challenge was that the letter had to be sent through the regular mail from your current residence and received within seven days. You were not allowed to overnight the letter or send it through another carrier. You couldn't even be certain that your letter had arrived in the United States! In 1994, the Green Card lottery consisted of fifty-five thousand visas issued annually worldwide.[1] You can imagine how many millions of people participated in this lottery. And it was literally a lottery. I sent my envelope in and hoped for the best.

One afternoon, while I was still completing my military service, my dad called me. He angrily asked me what I was thinking by making a purchase on the Visa credit card. When I was eighteen, my dad had given me a Visa credit card in case of emergencies. I told him that I hadn't purchased anything with the Visa card and asked what he was referring to. He told me that a big envelope came from Visa. I asked him to open it up and fax it to me. When the first page came

---

[1] "Registration for the Diversity Immigrant (DV-1) Visa Program," *Federal Register* 59, no. 62 (March 31, 1994): 0, https://www.govinfo.gov/content/pkg/FR-1994-03-31/html/94-7578.htm.

out of the fax machine, it read, "Congratulations, you have been chosen by the Diversity Immigrant Visa Program." I could not believe it! I was one of the fifty-five thousand individuals selected in the lottery to apply to become a Green Card holder. The next steps were to officially apply for a resident alien card, complete a medical examination, and schedule an interview at the US Embassy in Frankfurt.

"Your word is a lamp for my feet, a light on my path." (Psalm 119:105).

66 *I was interested in starting a business and employing Americans to help me grow the company.* 99

In December 1995, just a few days before a government shutdown, I went to the embassy for the interview. The lady asked me why I wanted to move to the United States, and I said I wanted to become an airline pilot with a major airline. She told me that many pilots were in the US already and that I would not have a chance to get a job there as a pilot. My heart sank deep down into my body, and I was horrified at the thought that I might not get my Green Card after all. Then, I told her that I also had my FAA airplane mechanic's license and that I was interested in starting a business and employing Americans to help me grow the company. I was so nervous I was throwing out words and hadn't even thought about what I was saying. *Where the heck did that come from?* I asked myself. In so many situations in my life, I have asked myself, *How did this just happen to me?* I actually have an answer to that question, but I do not want to get ahead of myself.

The lady was so surprised by my answer that she said, "Excellent, that sounds like a great plan for you." She asked me to raise my right hand, swear an oath, and repeat after her. An hour later, I received a sealed envelope with my name on it. My application and the approved paperwork for my Green Card were inside. She told me that I had to immigrate to the United States within three months from that day to receive my physical Green Card. I went home so excited to tell my parents about what had happened at the embassy. The next challenge was to figure out how I could immigrate within three months.

I had one ticket left from my apprenticeship at Lufthansa good for a standby, non-revenue ticket—essentially, a discounted employee ticket. Within three months, I managed to fly to Philadelphia for a very small fee and get a stamp in my passport.

GOOD MORNING, AMERICA!

I was hired as a first officer of a Beechcraft 1900 aircraft, the biggest plane I had ever flown.

There I was, on my journey of the unknown. I was so fortunate that the job market was open enough for me to get a job right away flying for a commuter airline called United Express. It was a feeder airline that carried passengers from less popular destinations to hub airports. In this case, the airline was serving the Minneapolis and Detroit airports. I was hired as a first officer of a Beechcraft 1900 aircraft, the biggest plane

31

I had ever flown up to that point. It holds nineteen people and has no flight attendants, which

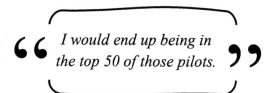

> I would end up being in the top 50 of those pilots.

meant I was the pilot and the flight attendant. Years later, I would return to Michigan to run an airplane manufacturing plant. Who could have guessed?

Flying for the commuter airline ended up costing me money since I had to fly there to work, plus I made less money as a copilot than flight attendants did. I decided to search for another job. I found a job in Texas flying a corporate jet for a lifeguard company. I also became the company's in-house mechanic. Without that mechanic's license, I wouldn't have gotten the pilot position with that company. I don't know how many times I wanted to quit my mechanic training in Germany and become a pilot because I was so impatient, but my mom always told me to tough it out and finish my training. I'm so glad and thankful that I listened to her.

After flying business jets with several companies, each with bigger equipment and more pay, I was finally hired by United Airlines. Yes, *the* United Airlines, for every pilot who dreams about flying 747s. I graduated from training in July 2000 at the age of twenty-seven. Back then, I thought I had made it for life. With United, once you're in, you're always in.

Calculating my age and normal attrition of employees at the company, out of the 11,700 pilots currently working on the seniority list, I would end up being in the top 50 of those pilots when I turned fifty-nine, one year before retirement. I was initially qualified as a flight engineer on the 727 airplanes, and then I became a copilot on the 737. It seemed like the greatest job ever. I was flying heavy equipment and making decent money; I saw a safe, secure career with a nice retirement in my future. Isn't that what we all hope for?

On the morning of September 11, 2001, I was at home, watching TV and witnessing the horrible events unfold. At that very moment, I knew that my aviation career as a junior-ranked pilot with the major airlines was pretty much done or at least disrupted for a while. The airline industry was not doing great anyway, but that event hit the entire travel industry. It was so devastating, especially because I became a US citizen only one month earlier to the day.

Over two thousand pilots, including myself, were furloughed from United Airlines within six weeks. I received $190 weekly unemployment from the government, which was still taxable. I immediately sent out hundreds of resumes to companies I thought would hire me. No luck. I was competing with more than six thousand other pilots who were also furloughed from the other major and commuter airlines.

One company, a simulator training company, invited me to interview in Dallas. They trained business aviation pilots on several corporate planes. I went in and was surprised by how intense the interview process was. First, Human Resources asked what I would do in this situation or that one and what the worst experience of my flying career had been. I was prepared from the interviews I had under my belt after years of working with the major airlines. I had gained a lot of experience and was able to tell real stories. Then I was brought into another room with real instructors. We had technical discussions, and they asked lots of questions about rules and regulations and my flying experience. Then the hiring manager for the department finished my interview process. One of the questions he asked was, "If you were recalled by United Airlines, would you go back?"

I replied, "I'm not sure how long I could be furloughed for. It could be six months or six years, but I would go back to my airline flying career."

At that point, he told me that the interview was completed and that I would hear from them. When I left the big simulator building, I asked myself why I told him that I would return to the airline. I thought, *How stupid of me.* After all, I needed a job, and they wouldn't want someone who was only committed to working a few months or years at most. I found out that six other pilots had applied for the one opening as a Citation instructor.

"I can do all this through him who gives me strength"
(Philippians 4:13).

A few days later, I received a phone call from Donna in human recourses. She was pleasant on the phone and got right to the point. She excitedly offered me a position as a simulator instructor in the Citation program! I was so thrilled about the opportunity. I was no longer unemployed and was finally bringing home a paycheck. This phone call changed my life again. Doors opened one after another and fueled my success in the aviation industry. I quickly became qualified in several other programs. Less than one year later, I had become a designated examiner for the airplanes, meaning that I could certify pilots to fly a specific jet. I loved my job.

I was naturalized as a US citizen five years after receiving my Green Card. I was so excited and proud. Ever since I was a young teenager, I had been telling myself that one day, I would hold a US passport in my hand. My dream had finally come true. You cannot imagine the feeling that went through me when I received this little blue book imprinted with my name, nationality, and the words "United States of America." It was the best feeling so far in my life. Exactly twenty years later, on September 11, 2021, I began writing this book. I would have never thought I would be a book author with the passion of adding value to many people like you.

A few years later, I was promoted to lead instructor, program manager, and head of training. I had more than twenty-five instructors working for me; it was a huge success to excel internally. I was sent to Brazil to be part of a joint venture between our company and the big airplane manufacturer Embraer. It was my first time visiting Brazil, and

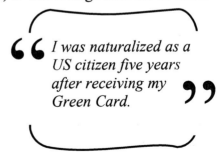

I was naturalized as a US citizen five years after receiving my Green Card.

I loved every moment of it. We sealed the deal and became the official training partner for their new airplane, the Phenom. The Phenom 100 was first introduced in 2008, and the Phenom 300 followed just a year later. I was lucky to be part of the initial instructors to fly, train, and examine new pilots.

My awesome team created the training curriculum for pilots and maintenance technicians. I regularly flew to Brazil, my passport was filled with stamps, and my international business experience increased. I learned from my superiors. I enjoyed my job and was even given opportunities to fly customers back to the US and Europe or wherever their home base was. I gained incredible experience from all the international flying.

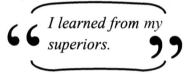

> *I learned from my superiors.*

"Choose wise and discerning and experienced men from your tribes, and I will appoint them as heads" (Deuteronomy 1:13).

It didn't stop there. I was responsible for the training centers in the United Kingdom and the US, and plans were created to add a training center for pilots in Brazil. An operation like this would be impossible for a single individual. You need the right people at the right place, which means that you have to have leaders at your locations running your business. You can't micromanage, but rather you empower your leaders. When you give your employees a great experience and treat them well, they go on to treat those under them well, and then ultimately, the customer gets treated well and has a great experience.

Customers liked the experience they received from me during the delivery flights from Brazil. I

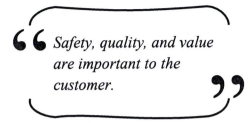

Safety, quality, and value are important to the customer.

received so much word-of-mouth advertisement that I had to take more and more vacation days to cover the extra flying work I took on. Safety, quality, and value are important to the customer, but the experience you give them can make all the difference.

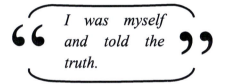

I was myself and told the truth.

Years later, I asked Tim, the manager responsible for hiring me, why he chose me instead of the other applicants. At this point, Tim and I were both at the management level; we held the same position in different departments and were responsible for different airplanes. He told me that every other applicant explained that they would never go back to the airlines. They were all frustrated and sour toward the airlines, and the events of 9/11 had changed their viewpoint. Many felt that they would never return to making good salaries or flying large, modern equipment. I was the only one who said that I would go back, regardless of how long it took. I was different from all the other applicants because I was myself and I told the truth. Tim told me that he felt comfortable hiring me for that position.

During this time, I began to receive inquiries from CEOs at various companies interested in my services. It was mind-blowing. The point came when I made another lifelong and life-changing decision, one that stretched me out of my comfort zone. It was risky and unpredictable. My parents questioned my decision. My dad even told me that I shouldn't do it because it meant giving up a secure job with a consistent income. The decision I was about to make meant that I would not have a stable income; I would not receive a steady paycheck every two weeks or clock in for a nine-to-five job.

I quit my full-time job to work as an independent contractor. I was independent of people making decisions for me and independent of other company's work rules, standards, and values. Now I was able to implement and use my standard, which was higher than any company I had ever worked for—a high standard of values, principles, quality, ethics, commitment, and happiness.

After teaching them all to fly Phenom airplanes, I had become friends with a handful of the CEOs from large companies, some in America and some in Germany. I won't disclose who they are for reasons of confidentiality, but industry leaders were in the cockpit with me who you have read about in magazines and seen on the news. I had so much fun, but more importantly, *they* had fun!

"Blessed are the pure in heart, for they will see God"
(Matthew 5:8).

They had the time of their lives, and I played a role in writing a small paragraph in a chapter of their lives. I am proud to have served them. Serving others

" Serving others makes me feel good. I become fulfilled when I can add value to people. "

makes me feel good. I become fulfilled when I can add value to people. Yes, I was burned a few times by being too generous and helpful, but after a while, I learned to recognize when I was being taken advantage of. Like a scorpion, if someone harms them, they sting back. If someone stings me, they fall out of my circle of trust.

Once you become the CEO of your own company, you must make a personal transformation with the goal of being successful. See, there are many excellent CEOs and even more non-excellent CEOs. But you must transform and switch from being a renter to an owner. You may ask yourself, *What does that mean*? It means that you change the way you think and value people; you begin valuing others before yourself. It's not that easy. It takes persistence, commitment, and dedication.

When you rent cars, you don't treat the rental car as you would your own car. You don't wash or detail it before you return it. You don't give it extra premium gas or bring it back after the rental time is up. You leave the trash behind because the rental car company will clean it. You get the point.

> *When you rent cars, you don't treat the rental car as you would your own car.*

Let's look at homeowners versus renters. If you rent, you probably don't change the filter on your air conditioning every four weeks or do the recommended preventative maintenance. You might be lax about scheduling landscapers to come and pull weeds out of your grass or shrubs. You might not pressure-wash your driveway and wash off the mold that formed throughout the seasons. You might not patch the little nicks on the wall or put a small layer of paint on discolored areas.

The difference is clear, isn't it? If you own something, you take care of it. Your favorite watch needs servicing every two to three years. You own it and don't just borrow it from someone. If you own a collectible car, you spend time frequently polishing and washing it. Think back to when you acted like an owner and when you acted like a renter. Do you own or rent your body? Do you believe your body is worth taking care of or that you are responsible for eating healthy and high-quality food? Do you pamper yourself often and get a manicure or a massage? Do you exercise? Do you meditate or reflect on how thankful you are for the blessings in your life?

"The Lord bless you and keep you, the Lord make His face shine upon you and be gracious to you; the Lord lifts up His countenance upon you and give you peace."
(Numbers 6:24–26).

> 66 *Every morning, you are given a chance to add value to others.* 99

Do you pray only during bad times or in times of need, or do you own your belief in God by also praying in the good times? Do you give thanks only during Thanksgiving or intentionally every day when you wake up and appreciate that you have been given a chance at life, a chance to make a difference in the life of another person?

Every morning, you are given a chance to add value to others. This is where intention comes in. Every morning, I write in a journal. I intentionally take five minutes out of my morning before I do anything else and give thanks. You have to be intentional to be significant. Every day, score a goal by making a difference.

Be intentionally thankful for everything you have and for your gifts from God. Start being intentional toward yourself by putting your goals first and focusing on your vision. Yes, it is important to put others first, but you need to know what you want in life before you can ever add value to others. I have lived in the US for twenty-seven years now. I came as an immigrant from Germany with very little money in my pocket, no friends, and no family. I had guardian angels by my side every single day, looking out for me, protecting me, guiding me, and most importantly, keeping me focused.

You can choose whether to play first and work later or work first and play later. I am so excited to tell you my story, a story of the American dream. Yes, it still exists, and you do not have to be an immigrant from Germany to live it. You are already here; you don't need to go through what I went through as a foreigner. It's time for you to unveil your potential, open your book, read your chapter, and walk your talk.

2 | YOUR INNER CIRCLE AND COMFORT ZONE

A mind that is stretched by a new experience can never go back to its old dimensions.
—Oliver Wendell Holmes

Insanity is doing the same thing over and over again and expecting different results.
—Albert Einstein

Coming out of your comfort zone is tough in the beginning, chaotic in the middle, and awesome in the end ... because in the end, it shows you a whole new world.
— Manoj Arora

In the beginning of December in 1994, I was a flight student in Saint Augustine, Florida, working on my pilot's license. Someone asked me what I would be doing over Christmas. I explained that I had no plans, and since I lived in a very small motel room, I didn't want to invite anyone to my undecorated place. You couldn't even sit very long on the hard wooden bench I had in the kitchenette. All the other students planned to return home to their families or were busy flying.

One morning, the pilot examiner, who had an office in the flight school, told me that I should celebrate Christmas with him and his family. He lived in Jacksonville, a fair drive about an hour or so up north. I researched where to go on the map, and since it was about a week until Christmas, I managed to find some small presents to bring. In Germany, it is customary to bring a gift for the host when you are invited to someone's house, especially the first time. I purchased a bottle of wine for him on Christmas Eve, and then on Christmas morning, I picked up a medium-sized flower arrangement at the local grocery store for his wife. I was surprised that the store was open on a holiday like Christmas, but I had looked it up the night before, and sure enough, they were open until lunchtime on Christmas Day. (This would be unimaginable in Germany.)

My examiner explained that his family would not eat dinner until about 6:00 p.m., so I planned to leave Saint Augustine at around 4:30 p.m., which would give me plenty of time. The drive was uneventful, and when I finally pulled up in his neighborhood, I was pleasantly surprised by the nice homes. As I looked for his house number on the mailboxes, I drove slowly and tried reading the numbers. A guy in one of the driveways was washing his car, and I was thinking, *Who in their right mind would wash a car on Christmas Day*? Well, come to find out, the number I was looking for matched the number of the driveway of the car being washed. To my surprise, I saw my examiner holding a sponge in one hand and a bucket in the other.

He looked at my car, and after I got out, he was surprised to see me holding the flowers and a bottle of wine. Maybe it was how I looked; I was dressed up, wearing nice slacks and a white button-down shirt. I walked up the driveway, and he smiled. "Sven! How are you? What are you doing here?"

You can imagine how awkward the situation was and how I felt. I said, "Don't you remember that you invited me for Christmas dinner? Did I mess up the time?"

He replied, "No, no, all is good. Come on in the house. I didn't expect you to come."

In the German language, we have a word *oberflächlich*, which translates to "superficial"—when people say something, but they don't mean it. Isn't it powerful to say something and mean it? Can you imagine how this story could have had a great ending with a completely different meaning? When you say something, anything, you should be careful with your words. Thirty years ago, we didn't have smartphones; we were lucky to have pagers. I call them the "brick phone days." Back then, we still communicated by voice and could hear each other's tones and inflections. The different tones we use will make a difference in the meaning of our words.

"Take control of what I say, O LORD, and guard my lips"
(Psalm 141:3 NLT).

45

Today, we communicate more and more with our smartphones and try to figure out what the other person meant to say when we read the text we received. Interestingly, we spend a lot of time analyzing the meaning and content of a text. Instead, we could communicate more effectively if we picked up the phone and talked to one another. Many of us have found ourselves trying to get the point across to someone after the fourth or fifth email exchange. Instead, pick up the phone and talk and explain yourself so that the person on the other end understands what you are trying to say. Many times, I have found myself in these situations of miscommunication before. We do not always feel comfortable communicating verbally; we would rather text or email. I'm telling you this story because this chapter is about your inner circle and your comfort zone, which relates to trust, dependability, and people having your back.

> *It would be more efficient if we picked up the phone and talked to one another.*

I have listed three types of friendship circles. Here is how I differentiate between the inner, middle, and outer circle of trust:

MY INNER CIRCLE

Your inner circle of friends is the most intimate circle of individuals who you trust. Those individuals are the main influencers in your life; they help and support you on a daily basis. You can totally trust and depend on your inner circle. Make sure that you have selected the right people in this very selective circle. They should not comprise more than a handful of people. God is one of them; my wife, the other; and two of my closest friends complete my inner circle.

MY MIDDLE CIRCLE

Different from your inner circle, your middle circle friends are those you like hanging out with whenever possible. They may come and go and enter and exit your circle frequently. Although these individuals are an important in your life, they do not influence your life's choices. They share common interests with you and may have the same opinions; however, they do not alter you on an emotional level. You may select certain individuals from your middle circle to become part of your inner circle at some point. This will not happen overnight; it is a process of maturing in your relationship. Remember, being part of your middle circle does not come with the same privileges associate with being in your inner circle.

MY OUTER CIRCLE

The outer circle is the simplest way of friendship. You cannot rely or depend on these individuals. You hang out with them at work, at school, or wherever you are with them. You greet them with "good morning" or "how are you?" and have casual conversations throughout the day with them. You do not share your innermost feelings and secrets with them. You may know these individuals through social media platforms but have never met them. We do not invest too much effort in them because we do not want to feel rejected,

47

embarrassed, or made fun of. Once you let these individuals deeper into your life, you might be disappointed by how they treat you. Sometimes you want to push the delete button on your outer circle friends, but sometimes you give them another chance to be part of your life. It is very hard for outer circle friends to move to your middle circle.

Here is what I have learned: Focus on your inner circle. That inner circle will not come tomorrow; it takes time, a long time, to cultivate. I call it the marinating process of friendship. A good stew will take hours to cook and only minutes to eat. Comparably, your inner circle is the same; it takes years or even decades of trust to let someone into your inner circle.

I can count the number of people in my inner circle on one hand. I know everything about them. I will do anything for them and go through anything for them. Most importantly, I can depend on and trust them. Look at your inner circle as part of your own family. Okay, I know that you cannot trust your own family in some cases—I get that. But you understand what I mean; your inner circle becomes your family even if you are not related. An important aspect of your inner circle is your spiritual circle. God (and my guardian angels) are the foundation and backbone of my inner circle. (I explain more about who my angels are and how they guided me through life in chapter 5.)

My friend Markus and I met on a bus on the way to a technical college in my hometown in Germany. I was a total introvert, shy and uncomfortable talking to any stranger as a child. I tried not to make eye contact because I didn't feel comfortable in any conversation. This is common in Germany, and as a child, you mind your own business. I got up in the morning, got ready for school, walked to the bus or train, sat with my earpieces in, and listened to music. I was so proud of owning a Sony Walkman and listening to music on a cassette. You might not know that a Walkman was the coolest thing around in the eighties. Anyway, listening to Michael Jackson was way better than talking to people, or at least, that's what I thought. I can't believe how different I was then from how I am today. I am the total opposite. If I don't talk to people in public, I feel awkward. I feel I am missing out on getting to know them. I take any opportunity to connect and network with people. How many friendships and opportunities did I miss out on going to and from school when I was young?

Anyway, every morning, that same guy boarded the bus and rode with me to school. For weeks, we had seen each other. We started connecting with a casual head nod, then we began talking to each other, and eventually, we became best friends. After more than thirty years, we still talk and are in contact although he lives in Germany and I live in America. Every birthday, he calls me, and we catch up on what happened during the year. And guess what? We don't take it personally when we don't hear from each other for months or until our birthdays—that's true friendship. We don't hold grudges against each other if we don't talk every week.

So what did it take to finally connect on the bus and start talking? After all, I was an introvert. I believe that we are all seeking common ground; we like to hang out with like-minded people. Think about who you hang out with: Usually, it's like-minded people with the same views and interests as you and not those who are opposite you, those you have nothing in common with. You feel more attracted to and comfortable with like-minded people who are just like you and your personality.

As the saying goes, "Birds of the feather flock together," and it is the same with people. For example, if you are from Texas, riding on a bus with your friends, and some New Yorkers are riding the bus, would you start connecting with them? New Yorkers have different personalities than Texans, speak differently, and follow different sports teams. Pretty much everything about the two states is different with little to no commonality between them, so no, you would not even be interested in connecting with them.

Now let's imagine a different bus in a different location. Now you are a Texan on a bus in South America, and you are traveling to a foreign country you have never been to. You feel lonely, uncomfortable, new, and insecure. All you hear is a foreign language, and you don't understand a word. In addition, the people look different; they are wearing different clothes, have different postures, different cultures, and act differently than what you are familiar with in Texas. Now suddenly, you hear English from the corner of the bus. This changes the whole picture. You tell yourself, *Oh my gosh, I can understand the person speaking!* You get closer to the people speaking English and discover that they are from the United States. It is refreshing to finally communicate in your language, share the same concerns, and have the same culture. Isn't it interesting that the standard goes from needing to be from the same state to being thrilled to connect with someone from the same country? In fact, the people you get along with so well on the bus in that foreign country are from New York.

Suddenly, you are quite all right talking and socializing with people from New York in South America, but you would hesitate to approach them if you met them on a bus in Texas. This relates to our attitude and how we view people. Why is that? Well, we need a safety net, a circle we can trust. With commonality, we start to trust people.

But we don't do this when we already feel comfortable; we do this when our guard is up, and we feel lonely, insecure, and uncomfortable. Has this ever happened to you? How did you react? How did you feel about it? Sometimes we need to lower our commonality standard to connect with strangers. When you talk to seniors about their memories and life experiences, most of them will tell you that some of their most beautiful and meaningful moments happened when they stepped outside their comfort zone.

As busy adults, we tend to slip into dullness and routine far too easily. We typically love the status quo. All is good—why change anything? Traveling to a foreign country is one of the best ways to step outside your comfort zone. So many people dream about traveling and living abroad; however, many will never do it. The fear of facing unfamiliar situations and experiencing culture shock discourages many from starting their journey.

POSITIVE CULTURE SHOCK

According to Verge Magazine, culture shock can be best described as "emotional disorientation characterized by feelings of shock and anxiety."[2] Culture shock happens when we enter an unfamiliar environment, far away from our hometown, family, and friends. Culture shock is typical at the beginning of a trip. Exposure to a new culture and new experiences can be frightening and exciting. Sadly, many of us have never even left our home state. Many of us don't even own a passport. Don't be afraid of traveling. Even culture shock can be positive because it opens you up to learning about yourself and your relationship with the world.

According to the article, here are some positive effects of culture shock.

In order to grow a thicker skin, we need to teach ourselves to trust our own gut feeling, which, in turn, helps us survive during challenging periods of loneliness or being in a unfamiliar situation.

People often experience tremendous growth when they feel vulnerable. In a unfamiliar environment, you might feel uncomfortable, scared, and confused. How many times have

---

[2] Ana Parfenova, "5 Reasons Why Experiencing Culture Shock is Good for You," *Verge Magazine*, accessed March 19, 2022, https://www.vergemagazine.com/work-abroad/blogs/980-5-reasons-why-experiencing-culture-shock-is-good-for-you.html.

we been in a large group where we didn't know anybody? We have to start making conversation with strangers. These moments will shape who you are as a person and make you realize what you are capable of. Yes, these situations seem stressful, but this exposure will help build your character.

Learning a new language might also be considered culture shock. It will force you to adapt and learn new grammar. My parents taught me the Dutch language first in Germany before I went to kindergarten, and then once I was in pre-K, I learned how to speak German. I'm so grateful for this. Even today, I can communicate in Dutch.

Knowing a second language is becoming a necessity in our world. Learning a language in a classroom is very different from immersing yourself in a new culture and learning the language that way. Language and thought are connected, so by learning a new language, you will start to think differently as well. Here's an example: I sometimes catch myself counting in German even though I'm here in the United States and think in English. Counting in German is easier for me than in English for some odd reason. Sometimes I still translate in German to myself while I answer in English. Our brains are an amazing tool.

Finally, you will have an opportunity to expand your circle of friends to include people from all over the world once you minimize the effects of culture shock. You become more comfortable in your new surroundings.

One of the advantages of traveling and living abroad is meeting new people and fostering new friendships. It is so important to meet people with different perspectives, backgrounds, and life experiences. This can be very transformative because it often shapes us into more open-minded people. Once you become more open-minded, many additional doors will open up on a personal and professional level.

I experienced many opportunities when I was living in Switzerland for three years. I walked through open doors, which I still benefit from today. Alternately, I have had the opportunity to impact other people's lives, and now they have a completely different perspective as well.

Traveling and living abroad makes you more open-minded. You may notice that people who have never traveled far from home are generally more close-minded than people who have lived abroad. When you expose yourself to different living or travel experiences, you gain mental flexibility and greater open-mindedness.

Never be afraid of getting to know an entirely new culture. It is a tremendously exciting and beneficial experience. When you travel or live abroad, you will have the opportunity to see things you may not see otherwise. You will have unique experiences and do things that you can't do in your home country. Imagine how exciting it would be to ride an elephant in Southeast Asia, travel through the rice fields in Indonesia, or explore the Amazon basin in Brazil. Exploring a new culture by discovering its music, trying new foods, and learning about the history and traditions of your destination not only enriches you as an individual but also offers a valuable life experience that you will never forget.

I have done many exciting things while living and traveling abroad and don't regret any of them. Just imagine how many lives you will also be able to touch and the friends you will make by traveling internationally. I have more friends abroad than in my home state.

I have come to the conclusion that traveling abroad truly reinforces the idea that we all share the same human experience. Traveling internationally will teach you the valuable lesson that this world is a small place. Despite variations in cultures, we share similar aspirations, such as love and joy in what we do, respect, protecting our families, and of course, earning a good living.[3]

Fear and anxiety often indicate that we are moving in a positive direction, out of the safe borders of our comfort zone, and in the direction of our true purpose. When you get out of your comfort zone, be careful to maintain a clear vision. Many of us get into trouble when we leave our comfort zone and then lose track of what we want to do. If you don't learn from your mistakes, then going out of your status quo life won't do anything to or for you. When I was a young adult, people told me that the only time I would grow in life was by getting out of my comfort zone and feeling uncomfortable. It doesn't sound like much fun, does it?

---

[3] Ibid.

We've all heard this famous quote by Albert Einstein: Insanity is doing the same thing over and over again and expecting different results. Well, the reality is that when you keep doing the same thing over and over, it is simply insanity unless you are learning from it. Are you enhancing your education? Are you adding value to people? Are you experiencing failure because you have done something that you have never done before? Have you messed up at your job and taken longer than typical on the same task?

My friend Mayra, who is an accountant, once told me that when she changed jobs, her new employer made her input the financial sheets differently than how she was previously used to doing it. The new way took her five times longer than before; it was frustrating and embarrassing. Is it even worth doing something a different way? The answer is yes. Changing the status quo is positive and a sign of both professional and personal growth. She learned a completely different approach to a solution. It made her more rounded as she gained knowledge and ultimately grew.

Is learning a new language easy? Of course not. Do you learn it overnight? Of course not. Does it make you more valuable to others? Absolutely. But most importantly, you will be able to add value to others. Why? Because now you can communicate to people who speak the same language as you do. If you only speak one language, you can only communicate in that language. Can you imagine how much value you could add to others by communicating with them if you speak two, three, or four languages?

By adding value to others, you add value to yourself. If you put others first, the focus is not on you but on growing others. See, when you grow, you have the potential to share your knowledge with others and help them grow. Helping others is what life is all about. Many people do not want to help others or add value to them. These people are closed-minded, insecure, lack a global mindset, and limit themselves and others.

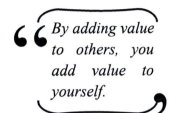

By adding value to others, you add value to yourself.

FAILURE IN THE COMFORT ZONE

When you graduate from flight school as a pilot, you know how to fly planes; however, you need to add experience by flying regularly. On average, professional commercial pilots fly between seventy-five and eighty hours per week and have ten days off per month. A newbie crew member has way less "real world" experience than someone who has been flying for years and years. This is true for every profession in the world. The longer you do something, the more you know and the more experience you have.

One exception to this rule is when you become too comfortable. Once a pilot gains a certain experience level, they must take a refresher class to requalify each year or so. Pilots need refresher courses because they begin feeling very comfortable behind the wheel of the plane. They forget to pay attention to details; this can be dangerous for a pilot and hinder their success.

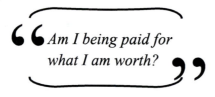
" *Am I being paid for what I am worth?* **"**

Most of the working class has the following mentality: go to work, do the job, try to stay below the radar, pass quarterly or annual reviews, collect a paycheck every week or two, and go home. I do this repeatedly. Then on Friday, I can't wait to say TGIF—"thank God it's Friday." This is very important: When you collect a paycheck, you are being paid for your time spent at work. We negotiate an hourly rate or annual salary, hoping to get a yearly raise, a bonus, or some sort of profit-sharing. The real question you must ask yourself is, "Am I being reimbursed for my talents and gifts? Am I being paid for what I am worth?" Have you ever asked yourself what you are worth? Is it about the salary or about something else? Look at the big picture.

All through my young adulthood, all I cared about was how much money I could earn. I made a good chunk of money because I believed in the principle of capitalism. However, it's all relative—the more you work, the more you earn, and the more you earn, the more taxes you pay. I am fine with that—are you? How many times have we complained about how much we pay in taxes? Have we ever asked ourselves how much money we earn? An increase in pay usually means an increase in the standard of living. When you don't earn much, you can't spend much, or at least you shouldn't because you will end up using credit cards and accumulating debt. We add credit cards or increase our credit limit, and at some point, we can't pay it back and live from paycheck to paycheck. Sound familiar? Do you want to change that? Are you willing to sacrifice your status quo; get out of your comfort zone; and grow personally, financially, and spiritually?

The answer lies with you, and I hope you join me on my journey to financial freedom and independence in your professional career.

You will fail if you stay within your comfort zone. Success is not a comfortable process but is very uncomfortable to navigate. You must become comfortable being uncomfortable if you ever want to be successful. Start putting some pressure on yourself to do just that today.

3 | FLYING ABOVE AND BEYOND AVERAGE

Don't take no for an answer and never submit to failure. Do not be fobbed off with mere personal success or acceptance. You will make all kinds of mistakes, but as long as you are generous and true, and also fierce, you cannot hurt the world or events.
—Winston Churchill

If I would have listened to the naysayers, I would still be in the Austrian Alps yodeling.
—Arnold Schwarzenegger

The purpose of a business is to create a customer who creates customers.
—Peter Drucker

Being above average is not hard. I once made a reservation at my favorite restaurant and thinking about eating my favorite dish. The hostess told me that the table was not ready yet, and it would just take another ten to fifteen minutes. No problem, I was looking forward to the great service I always get from a waitress named Bree.

I'm a regular at my favorite oyster bar in Florida, and many employees know me by name, which isn't hard if you have a name like mine. Except that sometimes people struggle with the pronunciation. I may be called Spam, Swinn, Fenn, Seven, Sawen, and the list goes on. I always chuckle when people try to pronounce it.

A bank teller once asked if Sven was my real name. With a laugh, I told her, "As far as I know, yes. It hasn't changed since I was born." She said that her daughter is the biggest fan of Sven, the famous reindeer in the movie *Frozen*, even spelled the same way. The worker was so excited that she could not even complete the transaction I came in for. I asked what was wrong, and she replied by asking me for an autograph for my biggest fan. I autographed a blank deposit slip and made sure that she knew I was not a reindeer, not even closely related to one. She was quite excited to make her daughter happy. I always look forward to going to the same branch to represent the famous reindeer.

Meanwhile, back at the restaurant, it was finally time to be seated. Our table was next to the kitchen where all the action takes place—I love that! Energy pulsates through the atmosphere, and the cooks are chatting and bantering with each other. All the action is part of the experience. This inspired me to choose an open-kitchen concept at Waco Kitchen, where I serve as the CEO. It makes a big difference when you are transparent with your customers.

When Nathalie and I were seated, we found out that Bree had the night off and a different server was filling in for her. In my opinion, no one compares to Bree because she takes care of the customers and interacts with them to make them feel special—she helps create that great experience. Once, she found out that it was my birthday and served me an oyster with a candle sticking out of the ice. I have never had a birthday "dessert" like that before.

I can't remember the server's name from that night, but let's call him Tom. He was not easy to get along with; he was difficult to understand and took a long time to take our order. He brought the complimentary bread out very late, and our drinks did not even come until after the first round of oysters was served. He was not on time for refills, and we needed to look for him to get water. We felt like a burden and were uncomfortable asking for anything.

Our food must have sat at the kitchen's pickup area for a while because it did not taste fresh and wasn't warm when it arrived at the table. This story may make me sound like a complainer. I am not a complainer, but I do compare experiences. Don't we all do that? When you have a certain expectation regarding the service and food and it is not met, you are disappointed. How many times have we been disappointed when we go somewhere? We expect a certain level of service, food quality, or atmosphere, and we don't get what we expected. We are disappointed.

FORMULA FOR DISAPPOINTMENT
A formula in life is expectation - reality = disappointment. This formula works everywhere: in your personal life and at

work with your boss, coworkers, and clients. It works at a restaurant, in a hotel, or on a flight.

When I was a pilot at United Airlines, we were usually assigned to a four- or five-day trip with a crew we had never met before and would probably never meet or fly with again. At the time, United Airlines had over fourteen thousand pilots, and I was one of them. I joke about it today because my employee number was my identity with the airline, so I literally was a number to the company. It makes you feel warm and fuzzy, right? Not!

Anyway, it was time to report for duty in operations at the Chicago O'Hare airport. I deadheaded (commuted) on a flight up from Dallas, Texas, where I lived.

Hundreds of pilots and flight attendants met at the operations center to meet their crew for the trip. We checked the maintenance status of the plane, fuel load, passenger lists, and most importantly, the crew list. We always looked to see if we were flying with someone we had flown with before; it was rare, but sometimes it happened. I checked the names on the manifest and didn't recognize the other pilot's name. When it was almost time to meet for the flight, the other pilot looked around for me. I saw his name on his crew ID badge and introduced myself. "Hi, I'm Sven, and it is very nice to meet you."

He was a little more than six feet tall and looked down on me as if I were a pilot from a rival airline. He spoke gruffly to me. "You are Sven? I was looking for a six-foot tall blond blue-eyed Scandinavian-looking pilot."

There I was, five foot ten, with brown hair and blue-green eyes. He was kidding, of course. After the ice broke, I formally apologized for not meeting his expectations, and we had a good laugh about our first impressions. It was all in jest, but you can see that we all have certain expectations. We hit it off for the next five days and had a great time flying together. I learned a lot from him, and we became close friends. See, you might expect something, but what you get in return is reality.

However, your reality can always be turned into a positive experience. That was one of the first encounters when I experienced a twist from a negative to a positive, from looking at the glass half empty to suddenly seeing the glass as half full. The water level doesn't change; you look at the level and determine that it is positive and not negative. We encounter these scenarios many times during the day. If you choose to have a positive mindset rather than a negative one, you will put bad experiences behind you more quickly than if you held on to a negative attitude. I will address attitude and mindset later in the book.

BEING DIFFERENT IS GOOD

My parents gave me the name Sven. It was a very popular name in Germany during the seventies when I was growing up. When I first visited America, I compared everything I saw to Germany: the houses, cars, weather, people, and food. I compared the way people lived and how much space people had. Everything was much bigger and much different than where I grew up. My cousin's name is Danny, and I thought it was such a cool American name. I had other cousins named Bob, Alan, and Rick, and the list went on of these cool American names. So I wanted to change my name to John when I moved to America. I love that name. When I compare all the popular names in Germany, such as Rudolf, Jens, Dieter, Manfred, Mathias, Andreas, Hans, Franz, Walter, Werner, Otto, or Heinrich, the names in the US are completely different.

Another example of contrasting differences was in the German military. When I served my one-year mandatory service in the Air Force, we had access to the US airbase where we met up with Americans at their officer's clubs and restaurants. As you know, in Germany, we have one of the world's finest and purest quality of bratwurst on earth. Well, I'm biased because, obviously, I was born in Germany and grew up with German brats. However, while I was at the airbase in Frankfurt, Germany, what kind of sausage do you think I ate? It was a typical American hot dog with ketchup, relish, and onions. You probably chuckled at this point, and if you have ever tasted a true and real German brat, these other processed sausages cannot even come close to what we have in Germany.

"And we know that God causes everything to work together for the good of those who love God and are called according to his purpose for them. For God knew his people in advance, and he chose them to become like his

Son, so that his Son would be the firstborn among many
brothers and sisters"
(Romans 8:28 NLT).

The point is that the grass isn't always greener on the other side, but it is different, and being different is a good thing! I have lived in the US for more than twenty-seven years, and I have realized that more people remember me because of my unique name as compared to others with a common American name. Honestly, how many people with the name Sven do you know? Or with the name Fritz, Hans, or Horst? If you feel as though you are different from others, I congratulate you! It not only takes courage to be different, but it also gives you confidence in the long run. People remember you for your differences. Now, this can be positive, but it also can be negative. How people remember you is up to you. In fact, everything that you do, for better or worse, is up to you.

DON'T ACCEPT NO

One morning, I was at the Executive Airport in Battle Creek, Michigan. I was walking on the tarmac with my friend and business partner, Dieter, the owner of WACO Aircraft. We were looking at an outdated hanger to expand the company. WACO operates at the airport and is the world's leader in handcrafted airplanes that provide the ultimate sense of adventure. One hangar, which would have fulfilled our short-term operational needs, was located right next to ours. We talked to the company's CEO and asked if we could purchase the hangar from him and take over the lease from the airport. It didn't take him long to decide; he gave a firm no. You can imagine how disappointed we were, but while we were walking back to our side of the tarmac, we saw a bunch of undeveloped dirt. We looked at each other and exclaimed that we would build our own hangar. It wouldn't be the same size as the hangar we were looking at; no, it would be bigger, grander, and more modern to execute our future business plan.

See, we didn't accept no as an option. How many times have you accepted no as an answer and walked away? We had the vision of where the new hangers needed to be, how big they needed to be, and how much value they would add to the local airport community. I suggested building a fifty-seat cafeteria for employees to get a warm, fresh, healthy meal every day as part of WACO's expansion project. I was so excited that we could plan a small dine-in location for employees. My philosophy has always been that if I provide benefits to my employees, they will give back. If you treat your employees right, then they feel valued. If you don't treat your employees right, they don't feel valued. Productivity is one of the direct drivers of value. You give and you get, but in reality, you give and then get back much more.

Try it. Help someone in your friendship circle who doesn't expect any help from you. That person will never forget that you did something kind for them. When you need help, the friend will return the favor tenfold. I have seen it repeatedly in the past years with my friends and customers.

When Dieter and I were driving back to the hotel, I looked at all the businesses next to our company. Hundreds and hundreds of people were working at the airport: maintenance facilities employees, air traffic controllers, university employees, the US National Guard, and the list goes on. At that moment, it clicked, and I knew that those fifty seats in our cafeteria would not be enough to feed all those people. I suggested we increase the capacity of our restaurant to at least one hundred seats. We both agreed and began planning for something that would be off the charts. My vision was to be different in every way. We had an opportunity to build and create the best airport restaurant ever: WACO Kitchen.

WACO Kitchen is a brand-new restaurant located on the second floor of WACO Aircraft Corp at Battle Creek, Michigan's Executive Airport. Their mission is to provide value to their employees, neighbors, and local and aviation communities by offering nutritious, homemade meals.

Every time a guest chooses WACO Kitchen, they will experience a brilliant fusion of American and European cuisine, freshly prepared by internationally trained chefs. All produce, protein, and dairy products are locally sourced and organic. This farm-to-table approach paired with the zero food-waste philosophy creates a healthy and guilt-free environment. Even the to-go orders are packaged

> " *All produce, protein, and dairy products are locally sourced and organic.* "

in environmentally friendly containers.

WACO Kitchen offers five main dishes served daily as well as a rotating seasonal menu. The seasonal menu runs through the end of the quarter and currently features a Korean pork taco made with the same delicate hand as the original WACO taco. Also included in the first wave is a crab burger that sells out nearly every day, as guests were told it wouldn't be for long. Dieter, the owner of Waco Aircraft Corporation, told me to be different than others. Being different is good and unique and makes us successful in every way. There is nothing average or equal to WACO Kitchen. That statement stuck with me forever.

INSPIRATION

The inspiration for WACO Kitchen stemmed from Dieter and me.[4] We both are passionate aviation enthusiasts motivated by adding value to WACO employees, neighbors, and the entire aviation community. Our goal is to offer reasonably priced, nutritious meals without sacrificing quality or flavor. We believe that we have accomplished this and then some.

WACO Kitchen offers one of the most unique dining experiences in southwest Michigan and is open to the public from the road or ramp. Second-story accommodations provide panoramic views of runway 5L/23R and large

---

[4] "About: Waco kitchen: New unique restaurant in Battle Creek," WACO Kitchen, December 12, 2021, https://www.wacokitchen.com/about.

observation windows into WACO aircraft production and service facilities.

CONCEPT

The concept for WACO Kitchen was crafted by Switzerland's culinary experts. After working as holistic medical practitioners for decades, the Swiss team understands the crucial impact a person's diet can have on their overall quality of life. Genuine hospitality and internationally acclaimed food and beverage service are their forte, all of which are evident the moment you step into WACO Kitchen. The restaurant is a new platform to raise awareness of our passion for aviation and food. Our guests have an insight into our production and service facility though the kitchen windows or large open balcony windows.

This concept ensures the use of fresh, in-season ingredients while offering a unique variety of options each time you visit. WACO Kitchen was designed to combine Mediterranean flavor with the beautifully rich American culinary culture. It is a wonderful fusion of European heritage with a cool and spontaneous American approach to food. Brooke Pembroke, my restaurant manager at the Battle Creek location hit the point: In everything we do, we want to create an experience that our guests have never had at any restaurant, especially an airport restaurant. We want our customers to have confidence that we're doing everything the right way, the way they would do it at home.

SERVICE

WACO Kitchen strives to provide an unparalleled atmosphere of hospitality throughout the entire dining and take-out experience. They are eager to share the carefully curated European-inspired creations with every

> *When you dine at WACO Kitchen, you have the luxury of utilizing the entire kitchen staff as your personal chef.*

guest that enters the dining room. Each dish is carefully balanced and hand-crafted. When you dine at WACO Kitchen, you have the luxury of utilizing the entire kitchen staff as your personal chef.

In January 2021, Waco Kitchen opened its doors to the public for the first time. Due to COVID-19, in-house dining restrictions were applied, and we could only offer curbside and pickup service. We saw this as positive because we could streamline our processes, operate the kitchen more efficiently, and give the manager time to prepare for the in-dining experience for our guests. This was the first time the team worked together in the kitchen. We hired new employees from several different area restaurants. A lot of established restaurants were devastated by the COVID-19 restrictions. Since we had never had in-house dining, we didn't know any better and adapted accordingly.

Never take no for an answer. The word "no" will never start any of my sentences or any of my answers; in fact, it doesn't even exist in my vocabulary. Two words do not exist in my vocabulary: "no" and "bored." If someone tells me that they are bored, I just shake my head and feel sorry for them. I work an average of seventy to eighty hours a week. I would love to take their time of being bored and add it to my week. Unfortunately, life doesn't work like that. Whenever you have a vision and see the finish line ahead of you, it's like participating during a negative marathon. You're wondering, *What is a negative marathon*? When you start on a long journey, it will take a lot of energy. You train and prepare your body, and then you train your mind. Every day, you tell yourself that you can do it. Repetition is part of the key.

A lot of people will tell you that you can't do it, that you shouldn't leave your secure job, and that it is crazy to start your own business. They will remind you of the uncertainty of success and the possible financial implications. We call these folks "naysayers."

How often do you think I heard from coworkers, peers, and even friends about how crazy it was to put a high-end airport restaurant that served European fusion cuisine in a town like Battle Creek, Michigan? For those of you who have not been to Battle Creek, it is a small working-class town, known as Cereal City since it is the home of Kellogg's headquarters. It does not have any high-end restaurants, especially an existing airport

> " *No other airport restaurant serves farm-to-table, European fusion, or even healthy plant-based vegan meals.* "

72

restaurant. I have not been to an airport restaurant that serves the kind of food we planned to serve. No other airport restaurant serves farm-to-table, European fusion, or even healthy plant-based vegan meals. We are different; we disturb the status quo. Was it a risk? Sure! In my opinion, the secret to a successful restaurant has three main components: location, quality, and service.

LOCATION

Do you have to have the right location? People come to your restaurant because they are curious about the location. At an airport, guests watch airplanes while they eat their meals. This creates a unique ambiance for the diners as they eat a meal while watching different airplanes taking off, landing, and taxiing around the tarmac. All the activity involves great energy. This niche market serves people who enjoy seeing something that they don't see every day; it is a special occasion for guests to escape their routine. Especially in these times, people were tired of being locked up at home and not dining out.

One of the main ingredients of a successful restaurant is, no doubt, the location. How many times have you been to a restaurant where the surroundings were just not quite right? For instance, you wouldn't take your spouse or significant other out to a romantic dinner at a sports bar where you could only see the football game on the overhead TV. The location helps set a restaurant apart, especially when the same type of food is available anywhere. This element is very important and part of the success of your restaurant.

QUALITY

The next component is quality. In my opinion, quality is one of the most important factors in everything I buy. How many times have we bought something that breaks after a few uses or a few days? Then we either return it or throw it away. We live in a throwaway culture; consumers buy cheap items, knowing that they don't last. We are completely fine with the fact that we throw an item away when it no longer works.

I grew up with a mentality of buying something of high quality and keeping it forever. You may pay a little bit more initially, but you can enjoy it for much longer. In the long run, it costs less to buy a high-quality item you will use for a lifetime, service it regularly, and do not have to replace it for years. On the other hand, you will spend more money on a cheaper appliance because it will break right away. When I was a kid, my parents had a washing machine they brought with us from apartment to apartment. It followed us wherever we went. I thought, *When will this washing machine fail on us so we don't have to take it with us every time we move?* See, a washing machine nowadays may last ten years, but when I grew up in Germany, we had one that lasted twenty-five years. I am on my fifth washing machine since moving to the United States.

The same is true for quality food. You need to offer the best quality food available. The best option is farm-to-table. At WACO Kitchen, we purchase ingredients exclusively from known sources. We take the time to interview our suppliers and personally look at their farms. We want to know exactly where our ingredients come from. How many times have we

guest. "May I help the next guest in line, please?" That's the first sentence out of their mouths. If you ask for a specific sauce or an additional item, the employee's response is, "My pleasure. May I have your name for the order, please?" See, Chick-fil-A does it right; you are valued as a guest and treated with respect. People enjoy coming back every single time because the servers are polite. This culture flows from the top down; the leadership at Chick-fil-A focuses on training their employees. They value their employees, and therefore, the employees value their guests, and the guests feel valued. Anytime we feel valued and appreciated, we like it. One reason people return to a restaurant is that they enjoy the attention. I'm sure you've experienced this, and I don't need to explain the contrasting ordering process at Burger King.

The leaders of a company need to be servants to their employees. If we as leaders in a business are not serving our employees, how can our employees serve and add value to the guests of the restaurant or business? How can employees make guests feel appreciated if the employees don't feel appreciated?

TREAT YOUR EMPLOYEES THE WAY YOU WANT YOUR CUSTOMERS TREATED

Employee retention is one of the biggest challenges for companies. Recruiting and training a new employee costs more money than rewarding the current employee. For example, at Waco Aircraft, it costs approximately four thousand dollars to replace an hourly worker and up to forty thousand dollars to replace a midlevel, salaried employee.

Replacement costs at Waco Aircraft are usually 2.5 times the salary of the individual. The costs associated with turnover include lost customers and damaged morale. The key takeaway is that a company's leadership needs to serve its employees, and therefore, the employees will serve your customers.

ADDING VALUE TO OTHERS

How can you add value to others if you don't value yourself? This is an important question you need to ask when you start your business. If you work a nine-to-five job, you are probably reimbursed for your time but not for your talents or gifts. You are only rewarded for your talents and gifts if you work for yourself, start your own business, and do what you love. You can't wait to get up in the morning to go and add value to others through your business.

Whatever it is, whatever it may be, you need to identify what you love to do. No one can tell you what you should do or enjoy doing. You are the only one who can make yourself aware of and identify your gifts. Ask your inner circle of family and friends what they see in you. Many times, they will tell you what your strengths and weaknesses are. Others will tell you anything to make themselves look good. Do you want friends to tell you the truth even though sometimes hearing the truth

> *No one can tell you what you should do or enjoy doing.*

about yourself is very painful and may hurt you? That's what real friends are all about—being open and honest with you.

A business owner's main priority is to make a profit, but the point is to focus on others and not on yourself. You have to start adding value to others before you add value to yourself. You need to be selfish for others, not for yourself. I know that this is easy to say and hard to do. I realized that a business should add value and give customers what they want. When this is the focus, you get a tenfold profit in return. Customers will recommend you, and you won't even need to do any marketing.

When I began my business as a contractor, delivering airplanes for owner-operators, it was not important to see how much money I made every day. It was important for me to make the customer happy and see them smile once the mission was completed. The customer hated to leave because we got along so well while we worked together. It almost seemed as if we were a team instead of the service provider and paying customer. One customer became two, and then three and four and five. I received so many recommendations by word-of-mouth referrals; I never had a website or did any advertising. I wasn't on social media, promoting my business, but customers kept calling me. I had so many referrals that I needed help covering my schedule. After completing a mission with one

> " It was important for me to make the customer happy and see them smile once the mission was completed. "

customer, he told me that he wanted to hire me for his business. I took care of many customers while I served as a mentor pilot for individuals who were jet owner-operators. Many of them became friends, and some even became very close friends.

Surround yourself with people who know more than you do. If you ever find a person who is better than you are, hire them. If necessary, pay them more than you would pay yourself.

You might have heard about the crab in the bucket. A crab is trying to escape the bucket but is being held back by all the other crabs. He is continually pulled back down, talked out of leaving, discouraged, and made fun of. Sound familiar? Have you ever wanted to go somewhere but were talked out of it, maybe by your family, friends, or coworkers? There is a reason people successfully talk you out of pursuing your dreams and vision. Otherwise, you would have already started your own business and hired people to work with you. But that's okay—that's why you are reading this book.

"Love one another with brotherly affection. Outdo one another in showing honor"
(Romans 12:10 ESV).

I encourage you to jumpstart your dream, whatever it is. As I said in my introduction, this book is supposed to *inspire* you. If I could accomplish what I have, you, too, are capable of doing it, I promise you. I have never been offered a job by a poor person, only from wealthy people. I have learned how to learn from more experienced people who have accomplished much more in life than I have. I am inspired by positive people and driven by those with energy. I am motivated by determined people who are focused and believe in themselves and their purpose. I have learned to avoid negative people who gossip, complain, have bad attitudes, and settle for the status quo. I am always looking for people who are different from me, bigger than me, more successful than me, and more accomplished than me. I am looking for those who are more experienced in aviation and finance, who are wiser and stronger spiritually, and who want to help me grow as a person. I enjoy hanging around people who value others, themselves, and me as a person.

> " *I enjoy hanging around people who value others, themselves, and me as a person.* "

Once you hang out with the right people, they will be like a spark that ignites you to do things you never thought you could do. That is how it was with writing this book. One morning, I was in a van on my way to the airport with my friends Kevin and Kathi. Out of nowhere, Kathi told me that I should write a book and share my stories with everyone. I told her that I had always wanted to write a book but wasn't sure how to start or how to compose it.

After my friend told me to write the book, I went to my mentor John Maxwell, a well-known author, and asked him how he began writing a book. He said, "I start by writing down one word at a time and then the next word and then the next word and so on." I laughed at him and said that it surely was not that easy. Kathi's husband, Kevin, is also an author and has written fifty books in under five years with several best sellers on Amazon. Kevin offered to help guide me through the process of writing a book. Of course, everyone has their own way of writing books, but I think he is a man of credibility and success who knows what he's doing and knows how to add value to people. I appreciate that very much.

When I was at flight school as a student, I surrounded myself with the best instructors who knew much more than the average instructor. I surrounded myself with people who were captains with the major airlines. I still hang around people with far more experience than I have, and I have been flying professionally for more than twenty-five years. My attitude is *you never stop learning*. Every mission, every flight, every leg of the trip, every recurrent training, I learn something. Every time I fly with another pilot, I learn something from him or her. I go to the simulator once a year, and I learn something new. Even if I only learned one small thing, it was worth going back for training. I have been back fifteen times in this specific airplane in the past ten years.

I believe a bad attitude will limit you, but an open-minded attitude will give you an unlimited attitude. One day on a flight with my friend and mentor John Maxwell, he turned to me and said that my attitude determines your altitude. I replied: "Is that why we are flying at forty-five thousand feet today?" We both laughed.

How brilliant is that? How many people say, "The sky is the limit"? I disagree with that; if the sky is the limit, then you've limited yourself. There is no limit to what you can do. It's up to you as to how you want to structure your future. Look at an airplane that is about to take off. The air traffic controller just cleared you for takeoff, and the pilot decides to put his hands on the throttles and push them forward so that the airplane accelerates down the runway and pull back on the control wheel to make the airplane climb. You are in control of your throttle and control wheel to make your future climb.

Look at a toddler: When they start to crawl and then walk around the house, what is the most frequently happens? They fall. They get up, and then they fall again. At some point, after practice and repetition, toddlers begin to walk, and that's true for every single toddler. Walking is in our DNA; we have this determination of accomplishment after we are born. I have yet to see an adult who does not walk because they gave up practicing when they were a toddler. So if this is the case, then that means anything we put our minds to at any stage in our lives, we can grab it, work on it, practice it, and then accomplish it.

I once sat down for dinner at the bar of a hotel lobby on one of my overnights. As you do, I started making small talk with the guy sitting next to me. He asked what I did for a living, and I told him that I was a pilot. His eyes lit up, and he replied, "Oh, I always wanted to become a pilot, but I never will."

Without hesitation, I told him, "Yes, you are correct. You will never become a pilot." He looked at me with surprise because I had confirmed his negative thoughts. I explained that he could become a pilot just like I did but he would need to change his mindset.

If you tell yourself that you will never become, achieve, or fulfill your goals, then how can you ever be better than those limits you set for yourself? Here are the three things we need to do if we want to accomplish something significant in our lives:

1. **THOUGHTS**
2. **DESIRE**
3. **PLAN**

THOUGHTS

It all begins with a thought in your mind, maybe a dream or an attribute that others have that you want as well. Perhaps you want to become more like one of your role models. There's absolutely nothing wrong with that thought. In fact, it fuels the drive in your mind. You must imagine yourself in that position. For instance, you may have a dream of driving a Porsche one day. You have it in your mind, you dream about it, you see yourself in the car over and over. To create a habit with your thoughts, you must use repetition and repeat those thoughts. Think about it in the morning when you get up before you do anything, then think about it throughout the day while you are busy doing your routines, and then, most importantly, before you close your eyes to sleep, visualize yourself driving that beautiful sports car.

When you do this every day of the month and every month of the year, you will become more aware of Porsches on the road. Try it out—think about the color of the car you want to drive, and I guarantee that the next time you go on the road, you will see more and more cars with the color you have in mind. You train your mind to become aware of something that you really want and desire. You train your subconscious to become conscious of what you want. That's really key to changing your behavior. Consciously doing something every day for three weeks will create new habits. I guarantee it.

Now you have to go one step further than just having thoughts in your mind; you have to act on them. What I mean is that you could then go to the Porsche dealership. Engage all your senses with the car: look, touch, sit, and smell. Look at the engine, the wheels, the windows, the stitching. Put your hand on the steering wheel and possibly even take a test drive. Once you respond physically to a want or desire, it will give you even more motivation; it conditions your mind to think about that one thing. Your thoughts are the first step; by changing your habits, you change your subconscious mind to be someone you are not or to have something you do not.

DESIRE

If you want something, think and desire it. See yourself as what you want, and believe in yourself. The stronger the desire is to be someone, own something, or do something, the higher your chances are of becoming who you wish to be. Why do you want to become a business owner? Is it purely to make money, or is it primarily to add value to others? The desire to help people must be much stronger than the desire to make money. Your priorities and your desire need to especially be in the right place.

You must be very disciplined to have the right desire. Many people do things for the wrong reasons, and usually, they end up being hypocrites. I hate to tell you, but it's the truth. To be a person of integrity, you need to do the right thing when no one is watching. You

> " *If you do want to grow in business, spiritually, or financially, you must change.* "

must consciously tell yourself every day that you are going to change—change your job, your habits, and your future. Change the people you consistently hang around. Ask yourself, "Is this person keeping me at the same level or lifting me up?" By changing your circle of friends and people you trust, you can move into the unknown. As we said, this means getting out of your comfort zone, and it is the only way you can grow in life.

Look at the little seed of a flower. The seed is underground and happy where it's dark and nurtured by the dirt and water.

The only way for the flower to grow is to push through the dirt out of its comfort zone and explore what's above ground. Have you ever looked at it that way? Why do you think that so many people don't change in life and continue doing what they're happy with? It's because they feel comfortable, and there's nothing wrong with that either. If you don't want to grow, don't grow. However, if you do want to grow in business—if you want to grow spiritually or financially—you must change, get out of your comfort zone, and change your status quo. Again, your habits determine who you are, and changing your habits is what you will become. How many times have we heard that change is coming? Many times, but words alone cannot change anything.

PLAN

What is your plan? How do you plan? Are you a planner? A plan will help you organize. When I was young and traveling around the world with my parents during summer vacation, my parents planned every single step of our trip. We knew exactly where we would start and end each day and week of our vacation. Yes, you heard right, weeks. My parents and I went on vacation for six weeks. We had big suitcases and were organized with packing our clothes, especially because we were gone for so long. Looking back now, I think it was crazy. But I loved craziness. I was never involved in their planning, but I believe I get my organization skills from my parents.

Since my mom received flight benefits through Qantas Airways, she always planned for flights when the economy class would be full so we had a chance to be upgraded to business or even first class. Flying back in the late seventies and eighties was different from flying today. People dressed up; they wore ties, sports jackets, and even full suits. The women were classy; they wore dresses and traveled in style. If you look at airline passengers today, you would think they are going to the gym or beach or don't have any decent clothes.

Every day was planned. If we were in Hawaii, we ate breakfast, went on our scheduled tour to see volcanoes, and then attended a show or visited the Orchid Gardens. I must say, I would not like having all these activities planned out today. When I go on vacation now, which doesn't happen that often, I don't want to plan anything. I take each day as it comes, am spontaneous, and usually like to be idle sometimes.

On the other hand, my parents were totally disorganized with finances. They had very few investments and were average middle-class employees. My mom and dad retired after working for the same companies for over thirty years, as a sales manager and an accountant, respectively. Both worked in offices and, luckily, in jobs that weren't physically demanding. As I mentioned, I got sales talent from my dad and a love for numbers from my mom. It is important to be organized.

Successful people start their day by meditating, being thankful for who they are and what they have in life, or praying to God. They do this every morning; it's a routine. It became a habit for me after a while.

RICH MINDSET VERSUS POOR MINDSET

The rich mindset talks about vision. The poor mindset gossips about people. Talk like the rich, and they'll talk with you, not about you.

The rich mindset focuses on their money making more money. The poor mindset wastes money on things they don't need. Spend money like the rich, and you'll be one of them. Invest in yourself.

The rich mindset surrounds themselves with like-minded people. You are the average of the five people you are around the most. Be around rich-minded people, and you'll become and stay rich-minded.

A rich mindset is proactive. The poor mindset is reactive. The rich mindset prepares for future problems; the poor mindset does nothing and complains later. The rich mindset doesn't help complainers; they focus on solutions and support you.

The rich mindset acts first and talks later. The poor mindset talks about acting but never does it. Be an action taker instead of a big talker, and the rich mindset will respect you forever.

How many books do you read? Do you read to learn and grow? Reading should be part of your daily routine. Even fifteen minutes a day adds up. Plan your day so that you can go to the grocery store for fresh, healthy vegetables and make a nice dinner, a healthy breakfast, or even a homemade sandwich for lunch. This takes scheduling and planning your grocery list.

Focus on adding value to people every day. Each morning, you should think of one person you want to add value to during the day even if it's a small gesture, such as calling a friend you haven't spoken to in a while, asking how they are doing, and telling them that you are thinking of them. Ask your neighbor if you can help them do anything around their house or pick up something for them from the store. Talk to one of your colleagues at work and ask how you could add value to them. If you are in a leadership position, plan to praise at least one employee an hour. You can touch ten people per day. A "good job" or "thank you for all you do" goes a long way and doesn't cost your company a penny. Remember how much it costs to replace an employee? A valued employee will value the customer as much as they are valued. Value is a two-way street.

Plan to meet people who are smarter than you. Try to meet those who are at a place in life or business where you would like to be. The majority will lift you up and show you how to start. Remember, on the day you were born, your book of life was already written. Your values and strengths were already predetermined on that day.

It was all written for you. Now it is time to open your eyes and read the first chapter, and then the next one, and so on. When we are ignorant about our values and talents, we will never grow. Take the risk and start reading. How? Every day, I close my eyes and pray and challenge myself to receive an answer.

"I praise you because I am fearfully and wonderfully made;
your works are wonderful, I know that full well.
My frame was not hidden from you when I was made in the
secret place, when I was woven together in the depths of
the earth. Your eyes saw my unformed body;
all the days ordained for me were written
in your book before one of them came to be"
(Psalm 139:14–16).

What is in your mind is usually what comes true. You attract what you desire. Some people tell themselves every day, *I cannot do this. I shouldn't do it either.* These negative thoughts lead to more negative thoughts, which attracts even more negativity. If you are positive and tell yourself, *Yes, I can and will do this. I will become this person. I will be a business owner.* When you have positive inner thoughts, you will attract that instead. I will go one step further. Begin to say "I am" statements to yourself. "I am healthy. I am financially wealthy. I am a business owner (be specific, e.g., I am the CEO of my accounting firm). I am adding value to others." When you do this, positive outcomes will come even more quickly. At one time, I listened to positive affirmations on YouTube every night. I had a notebook where I wrote down what I was thankful for, what I could have done to make the day more successful, etc. Every night for three weeks, I wrote down this affirmation: "I am attracting positivity, health, and wealth in increasing amounts from increasing sources."

Guess what started happening? I received refund checks in the mail, checks I was waiting for and had forgotten about. I was given more customers to fly around, earning additional revenue. My schedule suddenly filled up with more customer flights, and I sold airplanes that were sitting for a while.

I conditioned my mind to attract the things I wanted. I started driving cars I had always dreamed about, flying airplanes I had always dreamed about. I met people I always wanted to meet, and most importantly, I met people who purposely added value to me and lifted me up to the next level. To an extent, they inspired me to write this book. It is not enough to get to know these wonderful people; you have to plan and execute for the future.

I hope I have made my point about what above average is and why we all should be above average. Being above average is not hard as we figure it out, so let's start being different and impacting ourselves, our family, our friends, and our future. I'm going to close with this verse for you to reflect on:

"Do not conform to the pattern of this world but be transformed by the renewing of your mind. Then you will be able to test and approve what God's will is— his good, pleasing and perfect will" (Romans 12:2).

4 | UNLIMITED
ATTITUDE

The only difference between a bad day
and a good day is your attitude.
—Dennis Brown

There is little difference in people, but that little difference
makes a big difference. The little difference is attitude. The big
difference is whether it is positive or negative.
—W. Clement Stone

Until the mind is open, the heart stays closed.
The open mind is the key to the open heart.
— Byron Katie

Aren't these so true? It's back to the glass being half full and not half empty. It's the way you view situations in life, the way you choose to look at things every day. When people complain about the rain, I can't stand it. I think, *It's a good thing because the grass and all the plants need it!*

Other people say, "Oh, I wish it weren't so hot and humid." Isn't the grass always greener on the other side of the fence? When we consider our blessings, God works in us, which helps us be grateful for what we have.

95

Let me tell you a story about a wonderful luxury hotel. It's not wonderful because of the beds but because of the people who work there. If you walk by an employee, they say hello to you, not just because it's their job but because they truly mean it. You can feel that they care.

One morning, I went to buy a cup of coffee from the coffee stand in the lobby. The employee serving me was fantastic—funny, engaging, and friendly. I had so much fun buying a cup of coffee that I gave him a 100 percent tip. He was wonderful. I asked him if he liked his job, and without hesitation, he said, "I love my job."

Next, I asked him what the hotel is doing to make him say that he loves his job. He explained that his managers are supportive and check in daily to see how they can help him do his job better. Then he told me that he had a side job at a nearby casino where the managers micromanage the staff. He explained that they are constantly looking over the employees' shoulders to make sure they do everything right. He said that when he works at the casino, he tries to keep his head low and under the radar to get through the days so he can collect his paycheck every Friday. He told me that at the hotel coffee shop, he could be himself. What do you think? He is the same person, but a customer would have a very different experience, depending on where they were engaging with him.

Are you acting like the casino employee, keeping your head low, doing your job, and collecting your paycheck every week? If you are a manager reading this chapter, do you treat your employees like the casino or the luxury hotel? Are you focusing on whether your employees are doing things right, or are you responding to them with empathy and ensuring that they have the support they need to be successful? Many times, leadership has it completely wrong and focuses only on the people. But leadership should focus on cultivating the right work environment. If you have children, think about when they act up at home. Can you imagine putting them up for adoption for their bad attitude? That response would be much too drastic. It's not all about an employee's attitude; instead, it's about the company's attitude toward the employees—about being empathetic and supportive toward them a majority of the time.

"You must have the same attitude that Christ Jesus had" (Philippians 2:5 NLT).

Let's imagine that two workers—John and Michael—have the same job at the same manufacturing plant with the same pay, the same hours, and the same boss. John and Michael work on the same airplane and repair a fuel pump that brings the fuel from the wing to the engine. John is motivated, gets to his toolbox, and reads the maintenance manual on replacing the broken part. Michael is complaining about the fact that he must replace this fuel pump. He thinks, *I can't believe that I always have to fix things that shouldn't break.* Isn't that his job though? Rather than going to his toolbox and reading how to fix and replace the broken part, he reaches into his pocket and pulls out a cigarette. He thinks, *The company owes me some time. I'll just take a quick break.*

Seven minutes won't make a big difference. Besides, so many other people do it. I should be able to as well.

Again, this type of thinking highlights the difference between ownership and renting. We need to be owners and make sure that we treat our employees as owners and not renters. In the meantime, John has already figured out how to open the panel under the wing where the broken fuel pump is located and is helping his coworker find some screws on another airplane to put a different part back together. Additionally, John is thinking about contacting the manufacture of the fuel pump and providing them with feedback on how to improve the pump so it runs longer and doesn't break down as often.

What is different between John and Michael? You got it—attitude. John gets up about ninety minutes before he leaves each morning and can't wait to go to work; he looks forward to working on airplanes. Before he does anything, he opens his daily devotional and reads some lines about positivity and gratefulness. Then, he intentionally takes time to make a healthy breakfast: real oats boiled in almond milk for ten minutes in a nice porcelain bowl, topped with blueberries, strawberries, nuts, and granola. He leaves on time for work, and on his way, he's loudly proclaiming, "Good morning, world!" He is taking care of himself, treating himself right, and fueling himself with positivity.

Perhaps Michael forgot to set his alarm the night before and woke up fifteen minutes before he had to leave for work. His phone is at 3 percent because he forgot to charge it the night before. He doesn't have time for a shower; he jumps out of bed and throws on his work clothes. With no time for breakfast,

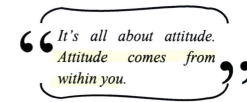

> *It's all about attitude. Attitude comes from within you.*

he rushes to his car and speeds to work. As he drives, he is cutting people off and yelling at them. He stops at the gas station to grab a coffee. When he's backing out, he has to slam on the brakes because he was not paying attention to the traffic, so he spills coffee on his pants. He angrily blames the other driver. He finally gets to work, but just as he pulls into the parking lot, one of his coworkers pulls into the last good spot. Michael is furious and so angry; he honks at his friend and internally blows a gasket, yelling and cursing inside his car. It's all about attitude. Attitude comes from within you.

I used to fly for a fractional airplane company that chartered flights to customers wealthy enough to pay tens of thousands of dollars to fly from place to place. I loved working every day and flying a modern fast Lear jet. I couldn't wait to get in my car and get to the airport to get the plane ready to fly. I was blessed to be employed by that company and to be the pilot of such high-end customers. I always looked forward to meeting the passengers because I had the opportunity to meet the people who could afford such luxury. I could converse with my passengers, and occasionally, I asked them how to get started in order to become successful. You'd be surprised at the answers I got; they were so simple that I thought, *If they can do that, I can do it too.* Their success wasn't rocket science; however, the majority were looking to add value to people by filling the needs within the market they served. Again, it is about serving others.

During one charter, our route began in Fort Worth, Texas, with a reposition to Tulsa, Oklahoma, and then to New York City. That totaled approximately a four-hour flying schedule with an additional two and a half hours on duty. My copilot for the three-day rotation was a man named Frank. He had come from another company where he flew Lear jets. When we first met at the airplane that day, I greeted him with a smile and the regular handshake and presented him with the flight plan, weather forecast, and airplane maintenance status report. Pilots perform these checks every time they fly and review the paperwork to make sure that everything is in order. Then we went to the airplane for a pre-flight inspection and ensured that the inside and outside of the airplane were in airworthy condition.

While Frank was doing the pre-flight inspection, I was sitting in the cockpit, setting up the flight plan and systems for departure. We had an empty leg (that's what we call it) with no passengers on our way to Tulsa for repositioning. The plan was to pick up passengers in Tulsa and fly them to New York. We started the engines and taxied the airplane toward the runway. As we were taxiing, air traffic control informed us that a little bit of bad weather was at the departure end of the flight route, and we needed to wait until they gave us the okay to fly.

Frank was looking at his watch as he told me how he hated waiting on the ground. I told him not to worry and that we would make up the time on the ground in Tulsa. Dispatch always gave us about an hour and a half between flights as a buffer to account for delays. The wait gave me the opportunity to ask Frank some questions about his background, such as where he was from and what he enjoyed doing in his free time. I tried to find similarities so that we could talk and connect as I commonly fly with pilots I have never met before. This also happened regularly with United Airlines, where it's even rare to fly with the same pilots throughout the year.

Frank was impatiently asking the tower controller if the airplane departures were going to be released. The tower told us to standby while they checked. A few minutes later, the tower replied and said it probably would be another ten minutes before he got an update. This commonly happens during bad weather. Frank was continually looking at his watch, getting more impatient and aggravated by the moment. While we were waiting, I managed to complete some of the required en route paperwork for the trip report, including filing flight plans for the second leg to New York and pulling the latest weather report for the northeastern portion of the US. I was happy to get a head start on all the work that needed to be done anyway. While I worked on that, I was thinking about where we could go for dinner that night. I grabbed a coffee from the back cabinet and asked Frank if he wanted one too. Aggravated, he told me that he wasn't thirsty and all he wanted was to takeoff. I told him that's what I wanted to do also but that we really couldn't do anything about it. It was out of our control. I encouraged him to make the best out of the situation.

Finally, the air traffic controller cleared us for takeoff, and off we went for a great flight to Tulsa. We had a couple of storm clouds ahead of us, and Frank told me that he hates flying during storms. I thought, *Why did you become a pilot if you don't like flying during storms?* As pilots, we never intend to fly into storms; we always circumnavigate around storm clouds, which we call "build-ups." I would never fly directly into a thunderstorm cloud intentionally. No pilot would. But to flat-out say that he did not want or like to fly when it's storming is like saying that you hate driving as a commercial truck driver and dealing with construction detours on your way to your destination. You deal with it because you can't do anything about it; construction is always going on. The weather in the airplane is the same. If you fly the same route from point A to B for five days in a row, I can guarantee you that you will encounter a different scenario every day. That's what makes flying so exciting for me: It's never the same.

We were given the approach clearance with favorable wind conditions to land on the runway. But this added a few extra minutes to the approach. It's called flying downwind leg, where you turn around 180 degrees so that you land into the wind, which is necessary for landing and taking off. Frank was going on and on, complaining about why they couldn't give us a runway with a straight-on approach. I explained to him that we would've had to land with a tailwind if they had.

I tried to present a positive outlook. "At least we have a nice view of downtown Tulsa."

We were asked to fill up the airplane with jet fuel after landing and taxiing to the Business Aviation Terminal, which we call FBO, which stands for a fixed base operator. Fuel prices were much lower in Tulsa than they were in Fort Worth where we departed. Frank again complained about filling up with fuel that morning since the company pays for it anyway. By now, I realized that I was dealing with a person with a great deal of negativity. I have a lot of patience, but at some point, it's too much even for me. I thought, *I will try to find out why he is in such a bad mood.*

We finally finished fueling and received all the catering boxes for the passengers: just a few snack boxes, including sandwiches and drinks. The passengers arrived with lots of luggage. The luggage was within limits for loading and size, but since it was a small plane, it was always a lot of work to try to puzzle the pieces into the small baggage compartment. I always find it challenging to fit in the luggage, like playing a game of Tetris. Typically, the line guys help guide the luggage into the base compartment, but it's ultimately up to the pilot to make sure everything fits.

At this point, I wasn't going to ask Frank to do it since he had already commented on the amount of luggage the passengers showed up with and suggested that we FedEx some of the luggage to teach the passengers a lesson. I told Frank to go back to the plane to set up a flight plan and prepare the cockpit for departure. At this point, I really wanted to serve the passengers, who were very nice, friendly, and happy to be on board with us. The line guys helped me put the luggage in the airplane, and in the end, it was not too challenging.

I gave a tip to the guys who helped. They thanked me, gave me a smile and a handshake, and wished us a safe flight. We had a three-hour flight to New York. While en route, we received a message from the company that our schedule had changed and that we had to work an additional leg after we dropped off the passengers. This was very common, and our schedule tended to be fluid. You never really knew where you would end up in the evening or where you would fly the next day. For me, it was an adventure. I didn't really care where I ended up as long as I ended up at home at the end of my three- or four-day rotation. That's the excitement of business aviation for both the owner and the pilot. The owner has the flexibility to do whatever they want and fly wherever they want, and the pilot gets the exciting challenge of creating the flight plan file and figuring out where and how we can make it happen.

I always say that for every problem, there is a solution. Frank's attitude was that there is an opportunity to complain about every problem. He had a completely different mindset and attitude. I could go on and on with examples of Frank's negative outlook from when we flew together. Same guy, same plane, same situations—just a different mindset with a different attitude.

How many times have we seen this with our coworkers? Frank had an issue with the weather, luggage, passengers, the airplane, the crew meals, the hotel, and his salary. Anything that did happen or could happen was not good enough for him. I believe that you can always make improvements throughout the day at home or at work. But if you view situations with a negative mindset and attitude, with a no-solution mentality, then you set yourself up for complaining, conflict, not being fulfilled, and even anger. No one can do anything right, and nothing is good enough for the situation.

I view situations in a positive way; I try to see the reasoning behind what's happening and put a positive spin on it. It's easier and more enjoyable for me to come up with a solution rather than come up with an excuse not to find a solution and instead complain. See, if you go above and beyond, you have an open mind for a challenge, and if you are willing to serve others rather than always needing others to serve you, you will have a much healthier daily approach to life. I consider myself very fortunate to be a pilot. Did it take a lot of effort to get to this place? Yes, absolutely. Did Frank have to do the same maneuvers and put forth the same effort when he passed his pilot's license? Yes, he did. Did he have to go through the same interview process as I did when he was hired? Yes. Does he fly the same airplane, during the same time, at the same place as I do, making the same trip? Yes. The big difference is how we choose to view situations. Frank looked at the glass as half empty and not half full; he looked at the day as an opportunity to complain. I look at each day as an opportunity to add value to people; I look for opportunities to find solutions and make life better.

Do you always have good days in your life? No, of course not, but it's not about the issues you are going through; it is about how you handle them. The best way to handle difficulties is with your attitude. How you will deal with the situation is up to you; you can either choose to look at the situation as a problem with an opportunity to complain or you can see a problem as an opportunity to find a solution. Choose to be a problem solver with a positive attitude; I guarantee that it will make you much healthier in your mind and attract like-minded people to you.

BIRDS OF A FEATHER

Do you feel comfortable around like-minded people, those who act similarly to how you act? If you are a positive person with a positive perspective, regularly in a good mood, and you like to add value to people, then most likely, you do not enjoy hanging out with complainers who are negative and who have no drive. I certainly don't. I don't feel comfortable around these people, and they bring me down. If you are hanging out with people who are not like-minded, then either *you* have to change, or you have to change your friends. If you have a great attitude and want to grow but have friends who are satisfied with the status quo and do the same thing repeatedly every day, they will try to talk you out of going into an area of uncertainty, such as growing a business. If you are experiencing this, then you need to let go.

106

Remember that "Birds of a feather flock together." If you have naysayers in your life, those who hold you down, don't share your dreams, discourage you, or make it hard for you to change, then it's time to cut ties with them and move on. That's one of the hardest decisions you must make in life. Life is way too short not to do good for yourself and, most importantly, for others. If you don't have the right environment around you, you must decide to change it. Remember, your book of life was already written before you were born. Open your book, read your chapter, and act on what's been written for you.

OPEN-MINDED

To have an open mind means to be willing to consider, entertain, and implement new and diverse concepts.

Being open-minded involves being receptive to a wide variety of viewpoints and ideas. Open-minded people are willing to change their views when presented with new facts and evidence.

EMBRACE THE UNKNOWN

You can't foresee everything in life. Sure, this may sound a bit general, but the unknown can really mean something as simple as taking a different route to work, accepting that lunch date with your neighbor, or watching a movie by an actor you've never heard of. If you want to be more open-minded, then the first step is to embrace something completely foreign to you.

Have you decided not to check out the new restaurant in town because you don't know what it's like there? Now's the time to check it out. Have you avoided signing up for that computer class you're interested in because you don't know anything about electronics? Go for it. Have you shied away from joining a fitness class? Take a beginner's class to help you get comfortable. Keep an open mind about things you've never done before.

Close-minded people often feel negatively toward things that they may have never even tried or experienced. If you have a negative mindset toward something, ask yourself if you have any experience to back up the negative thought. Try to learn more about subjects you are unfamiliar with: different foods, books, a health regimen, or religion.

Here are some practical steps to help you become more open-minded.[6]

SAY YES TO MORE INVITATIONS

Although you cannot always say yes to every invitation you get, however, you can make a habit of saying yes at least 50 percent of invites and accept invites to places you have never been before: a neighborhood potluck lunch, your friend's semiannual barbecue that you always skip, or even a Sunday Bible study that your husband has been trying to get you to attend for a while. Exposing yourself to a wide variety of events will make you more open-minded.

---

[6] Sandra Possing and Hannah Madden, "How to Be Open-Minded," Wikihow, last updated August 25, 2021, https://www.wikihow.com/Be-Open-Minded.

How about accepting invitations to different types of events? Just saying yes to party invitations may not necessarily broaden your horizons if you say no to everything else. The next time you say no to something, ask yourself what lies behind it: fear of the unknown, an unwillingness to step out of your comfort zone, or the desire to hang out at home on your cell phone instead of meeting new people? Face the feeling and find a way to fight it.

SWITCH YOUR PERSPECTIVE

We have to be aware that other people have opinions too and accept that. This counts for almost anything in life: politics, religion, personal beliefs, education, etc. You don't need to change your morals or views but try to see things from the other side. You'll become more open-minded and learn how to put yourself in someone else's position. Let's say, for instance, that you are a spiritual Christian. Can you try reading up on other religions or understanding the reasons why someone might not believe in God? Make a list of these reasons to see if it makes it easier for you to understand different perspectives. That does not mean you have to change your view, but this attitude will help you be more open-minded.

PRIME YOUR POSITIVITY

Too many close-minded people view things in a negative light. The next time a negative thought crosses your brain or escapes your lips, counteract it with a positive thought. It might help to think of three positive things for every one negative thought you have. Let's say you catch yourself saying, "It's freezing today. This weather sucks." Can you think of anything good about the cold day? Try "But there's nothing like drinking nice honey-flavored coffee at my favorite café when it's cold outside." Or "Maybe it'll snow later. I love to see the kids play in snow."

"Blessed are the pure in heart, for they will see God" (Matthew 5:8).

You can find the good in almost any situation. Maybe you hate your one-hour commute to work, but you love the alone time you get to listen to your favorite audiobook or music.

STIR UP YOUR ROUTINE

Break your old habits and try something new. Maybe eat an açai bowl for breakfast instead of steak and eggs. Take the subway to work rather than your car. Better yet, try carpooling. Getting out of a rut can really help open your mind and help you start creating new habits.

Routines are a great way to bring order and stability to your life, and there's nothing wrong with them. But if you want to be more open-minded, mixing it up occasionally will show you that there's more than one way to live your life. Let's say you planned to stay in all weekend and binge watch that TV show. Your friend invites you to his beach house at the last minute—if you want to start changing your life for the better and be more open to new experiences, then you might want to say yes.

READ MORE BOOKS

Pick a variety of topics and just dive in. You should read widely: non-fiction, documentaries, magazines, devotionals, the Bible, and anything else. Read a book about a country you've never been to or a book about nutrition you don't know much about. The more you know, the more power you'll have to make educated decisions and become more open-minded.

Start an online reading account and try to read at least two to three books a month. See what other people are reading and get inspired. Spend time at your local bookstore or the library, checking the shelves until you find a book that speaks to you. Then make a goal to finish it by the weekend. Join an online book club or find one in your area. This will open you up even more open to a wide variety of literature and will expose you to several new opinions.

TRAVEL FREQUENTLY

Open your mind to new experiences and cultures. Many people have a limited budget; however, you should make a habit of traveling when you find spare money. If you only have a little bit of money to spare, just travel to a fun destination a few hours away from your hometown and try to learn something new. If you have more money to work with, go to the pyramids in Egypt, check out the museums in Paris, or spend a weekend in Vancouver. If you can't afford to travel, watch the Travel Network. Though it won't be as exciting as the real thing, it will give you more perspective as to how people live in other countries.

GET UNCOMFORTABLE

Get out of your comfort zone! Choose something you're afraid of and try it. Many of my friends asked me to skydive with them. I am absolutely mortified of jumping out of an airplane that is completely airworthy and not about to crash. I am a pilot; why would I jump out of an airplane if it's not about to crash? I still have this on my to-do list. If you hate going to noisy restaurants, make a dinner reservation and see how it goes. Are you afraid of meeting new people? Let a friend drag you to a party. Make a habit of doing this as often as you can, and you'll slowly feel your mind opening up.

Here is a challenge for you. Write down five things that make you really uncomfortable. Find a way to do as many of these as you can. This will take time and courage, but you'll feel better for it!

1._____

2._____

3._____

4._____

5._____

"Have I not commanded you? Be strong and courageous.
Do not be frightened, and do not be dismayed, for
the Lord your God is with you wherever you go"
(Joshua 1:9).

JUDGE OTHERS CAREFULLY

Pre-judging someone can close a relationship or friendship before it even starts. That doesn't mean you can't discern. You have to know the difference between right and wrong. Try to keep your opinion neutral until you actually speak with someone and get to know them more. Even if you've heard about them from a friend, you don't really know much about them until you talk to them yourself and get to know them. Thirty years ago, when I first met one of my best friends today, I judged him. After hanging out with him and spending quality time together, I realized how wrong I was about my initial judgment of him. Don't close friendships only because you pre-judge others.

"Do not judge, or you too will be judged"
(Matthew 7:1).

The next time you meet a new person, try to understand where they're coming from before you form an opinion about them. If they talk loudly, maybe they're used to being ignored or looked over. Or maybe they even have a hearing problem, like my mom. If they seem standoffish, they might just be anxious or shy. When you're meeting a friend of a friend, consider that if your friend likes this person, then there should be something good about them. Try to find out.

ASK PROBING QUESTIONS

Learn something new from everyone you meet. You can do this with an old friend or someone you've never met before. Ask them what they've been up to, if they've read anything interesting lately, or about their last vacation. The more interested you are in other people's lives, the more you'll learn from them.

If you know the person well, ask them something personal, such as about their childhood. You may hear some really interesting details and learn something new.

Make new friends from different backgrounds. Increase your friendship horizons to gain different perspectives. It's fine to keep your close friends that you've known for years and years but try to branch out a little as well. Make friends from work, your yoga class, your favorite neighborhood restaurant, or from different classes in school. Though you shouldn't handpick your friends based on their diversity, try to hang out with people that have a variety of jobs, interests, and backgrounds and are more successful than you.

Questions are a simple but powerful way to connect with another person, help them to open up, and learn from them. One of my mentors asks these ten questions to people he wants to get to know better. (You can modify these for your use as well.)

1. What is the greatest lesson you have learned?
2. How has failure shaped your life?
3. What are your strengths?
4. What is your passion?
5. Who do you know I should know?
6. What book have you read that I should read?
7. What have you done I should do?
8. Can I express gratitude to you?

9. Will you speak honestly into my life?
10. Is there any way I can add value to you?

This last question is the most powerful one you can ask, and if they answer you, you had better have a plan to execute—that's the success formula.

5 | DISCOVER YOUR FAITH

Life begins at the end of your comfort zone.
—Neale Donald Walsch

Once we except the limits, we go beyond them.
—Albert Einstein

Success is not the key to happiness. Happiness is the key to success. If you love what you are doing, you will be successful.
—Albert Schweizer

When I was a young teenager in Germany, every Sunday, my dad went to church with me at the Frankfurt Dom, a big cathedral in Frankfurt built in the seventh century and completed in 1550. The large center of the main building was so silent. Thinking about it now, the smell of frankincense floated through the air and reminds me of when I was part of the eleven o'clock service as an altar boy.

Back in the eighties, it was not usual for a fifteen-year-old to serve as an altar boy. The term "altar boy" was somewhat controversial and often made fun of. I was in a group of about fifteen servers who met at church every weekend.

"Whoever is kind to the poor lends to the Lord, and he will reward them for what they have done"
(Proverbs 19:17).

Even then, I had a strong urge to serve others and loved the feeling. Once a month, we also served a meal to the

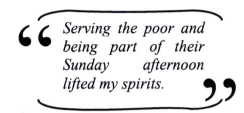

Serving the poor and being part of their Sunday afternoon lifted my spirits.

homeless after the service. Looking back, I was so proud of serving the homeless and giving out a warm meal and drink. I found it intriguing to talk to the guests of the kitchen. I met people who had struggled with drug addiction and lost jobs and homes due to family disputes and for many other sad reasons. Serving the poor and being part of their Sunday afternoon lifted my spirits.

If you had told me back then that I would be serving thousands of people every day through my restaurant, I would not have believed you. Adding value to people is rewarding in so many ways. It doesn't matter who you are serving; it is about being a servant to others. It will cause you to be humble and put your life into perspective.

I was a simple receiver in many ways but not yet a spiritual receiver. When I was involved with the church in my early days in Germany, my body served the community, the congregation, and the church staff. Once, the staff invited me for a cup of tea in the church's administration building. What was not present with me, however, was my spiritual body.

"And whatever you do, whether in word or deed, do it all in the name of the Lord Jesus, giving thanks to God the Father through him"
(Colossians 3:17).

Yes, I believed in God, Jesus, and the Bible, but I had no proof. As a kid, I needed proof of something to make me really believe that Jesus is real and that a God created us.

When you are present in church, there is a difference between your body and your spirit. This is a game-changer and very important to understand. If you can grab hold of this truth, you will move forward in this chapter and be immersed in the Holy Spirit. I hope you do because it changed my life when I discovered the difference.

Learning the truth made me grateful for what I have that others don't. It made me grateful for my health. Earlier, I explained why you shouldn't compare yourself with others; however, in this case, it is healthy to do so. Gratitude makes you realize many things and identify who you are and where you want to go in life. To grow, you need to know differences between you and

When you are present in church, there is a difference between your body and your spirit.

others, which you can use to add value to you and them. This is well worth it. This self-reflection made me aware that I took my parents for granted. I expected a lot from them when I was young. I frequently disrespected their time and energy.

"For all those who exalt themselves will be humbled, and those who humble themselves will be exalted"
(Luke 14:11).

I have always loved my parents, but comparing the past with the present has made me realize that the love from your parents is priceless and that any currency of the world could not repay everything they have done for me. This has made me appreciate parents who loved me like that. I know some households only have one parent, and you should hold your single parent, mom or dad, in the same esteem as if both were there. What about your spiritual Father? Have you ever thought of Him or been thankful for Him? Have you ever thought about how much He loves you?

As a child (and even as an adult), your parents might tell you exactly what to do and what not to do. "Sven, you will go to this school. Sven, you will join the soccer team. Sven, you will go on vacation with us. Sven, you should do this, that, and the other." I still remember those moments today. Good or bad, the point is that our parents always want the best of us. They want to mold us. They want to grow, nurture, and support us.

"We love because he first loved us"
(1 John 4:19).

119

I have news for you: Our spiritual Father does the same. He also wants to grow, nurture, and support us. The very day we were born, our book of life was written. Our destiny was defined. You were equipped with gifts, values, and talents on your first day of life. He looked at you and was so proud of what He created. He wants the best for us, and the most important thing is that His love is unconditional.

You may wonder, *What changed in Sven? What made him a spiritual receiver now but not back when he was a teen*? Some people may say that they got "saved"; others may have a different life experience that changes how they live and see life. In my case, my spirituality began the day my maternal grandfather passed away. His name was Hermann. He lived in Indonesia, and although we met several times when I visited there or he visited our family in Europe, I did not see him too often. As a child, I didn't like Asia that much. The food was so different; it looked and tasted weird to me. It was a third-world country, and the houses were built like it was. The sun's heat, the high humidity, and my inability to communicate with people made it a less than ideal vacation spot. I always looked up to my grandfather. He was tall, had flawless hair, dressed well, and was funny. Grandfather Hermann spoke with authority, and I admired many things about him.

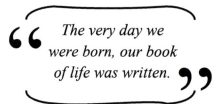

" *The very day we were born, our book of life was written.* "

One night as a child, I woke up already upright and standing outside on my balcony. I do not sleepwalk and never have, but that night, I did, and it really scared me. My eyes were already open. I was facing east, in the direction of Indonesia. I was so shocked but went back to my bed and tried to go back to sleep. The next morning, after I woke up, I joined my parents for breakfast in our small kitchen. I was so embarrassed about what had happened during the night that I didn't even share it with my parents. The phone rang, and my mom answered it in the living room. It was her sister calling her from Indonesia. My mom returned to the kitchen with tears in her eyes. She told my dad and me that my grandfather Hermann passed away several hours earlier. In that specific moment the night before, when I woke up sleepwalking, I knew that he wanted to say goodbye to me. He didn't want me to worry that he had passed. All would be well. I never heard any voices, but I knew that this was what he was telling me.

"Do you not know that your bodies are temples of the Holy Spirit, who is in you, whom you have received from God? You are not your own"
(1 Corinthians 6:19).

At that time, I did not know the impact and power of the Holy Spirit, but it was my first spiritual encounter, and it was life changing. The connection I had with my grandfather has helped me throughout my life. The memory that I carried of him and the power of that spiritual experience kept me out of trouble, pushed me in the right direction when I had important decisions to make, and protected me during dark moments in my life. I am writing this with tears in my eyes right now because I feel God's presence next to me, and I know that He has always been with me. Let me tell you, the presence of the Holy Spirit has no limitations. I can attest to this because I am flying at forty-three thousand feet over the desert of Texas at this very moment.

MY BOGOTÁ EXPERIENCE

I am not basing everything on this one encounter I had as a youth; that was merely the beginning. Here is the powerful story that proved that God is real and His Spirit is alive.

In March 2011, I was piloting a Phenom 100 with my dear friend Jerry. I met him about a year before our flight and was in the process of mentoring him to become a captain for the Phenom 100. Jerry was an owner-operator, which means he didn't fly for a living, but he was acquiring the skills to become a jet pilot in the Embraer aircraft. Unlike most other jets, it is a single-pilot airplane, which means you can fly it all by yourself without a copilot. We were flying from Ohio to Bogotá, Columbia. On the way down, we stopped in the Dominican Republic and picked up a pastor named John. It was a fairly long flight, and we needed to make a fuel stop anyway.

It was Jerry's first jet, and I was at his side during his simulator and aircraft training. After he graduated in the simulator, we flew many hours together so that he would be comfortable and proficient as a single pilot. He is not only a quick learner but also a great pilot, and after a few months of knowing him, we became friends. Jerry introduced me to many business leaders, famous book authors, and, of course, to his inner circle of spiritual leaders. All these things were new to me: praying before we ate a meal, giving thanks to God in the car out loud, and meeting like-minded Christians who prayed and worshipped God together in a very special way.

We landed in Bogotá, Columbia after a long but uneventful journey in his beautiful airplane. After checking into the hotel, I found out that I would be sharing a room with Pastor John. I had never met John or even heard of him before. He explained that he was a pastor from Toronto at Catch The Fire Church. The Holy Spirit touched millions of believers at this church. Here is the incredible story:

In January 1994, this little church of 360 regular members met on the end of a runway at Pearson International Airport in Toronto. It quickly came to the world's attention as a place where God chose to meet with His people as the Holy Spirit was poured out in unprecedented ways. As a result of this divine visitation, the members of what was at that time the Toronto Airport Vineyard were thrust into ministry to thousands of people worldwide. What was originally planned as a series of four meetings exploded into a marathon of nightly services that continued for over a decade.

The revival came to be known as the Toronto Blessing, with prolific media coverage all around the world. Within the first two years alone, almost one million guests had come through the doors of the church from virtually every country and denomination. Tens of thousands of people made a first-time commitment to Christ, and church membership increased exponentially.

The original 425-seat facility became overextended by the summer of 1994. Waiting lines formed at five o'clock outside the doors, which opened at seven. In November 1994, a former conference center on Attwell Drive became available for rent and later became the permanent home of Catch The Fire.

The effects of the Toronto Blessing quickly became international in scope. Within a year of the outpouring, an estimated four thousand churches representing main denominations in the United Kingdom were touched by the renewal and were holding their own nightly meetings. The Toronto Blessing spread not only to England but to hundreds of nations around the world, and the global impact has been immeasurable.[7]

On the evening of our arrival in Columbia, we went to a local church service with Jerry, John, and the local church leadership team. (I firmly believe God brought my path to Jerry, which led me to John and my Bogotá experience.) After the service, we gathered in the green room to introduce the team and for a briefing on our next stops in Columbia. The room was so cold; the air conditioning blew freezing air down my back. About fifteen people were in the room, and we all sat at a big conference table.

---

[7] "Who We Are," Catch The Fire Mississauga, accessed December 13, 2021, https://ctfmississauga.com/about-us.

"May the God of hope fill you with all joy and peace as you trust in him, so that you may overflow with hope by the power of the Holy Spirit"
(Romans 15:13).

The first person introduced himself, and after a short introduction, John prayed over him in front of the team. While John was praying for the person, everyone bowed their heads and closed their eyes. I was in the middle of the group, and about five people were ahead of me, introducing themselves. The closer it got to my turn, the more nervous I became. I didn't know anyone, and I was unsure of what to say about myself, and I was so uncomfortable due to the cold air. On top of that, I thought about what John would say when he prayed for me.

When my turn came, I rather quickly introduced myself and told the group how I was helping Jerry to become qualified in the aircraft. John prayed over me, and while he was touching my head with his left hand, I no longer felt cold. I became comfortably warm and completely stopped shivering. I was immersed in his words, and energy transferred from his hand into my whole body. It is very hard to explain exactly how it felt, but it was something real that I had never before experienced.

After a few minutes of this amazing experience of energy flowing through my head into my body, John finished his prayer over me. The person next to me began to introduce themselves, and the room started to become cold again. Once we all finished the introduction and prayers of the group, we had a nice dinner together. Then we drove to the hotel, and everyone went to their rooms for the evening. John and I entered the room, and I could not wait to ask him about my experience when he prayed for me. "John, how did you do that? The room suddenly became warm and cozy. I wasn't cold. What exactly did I feel when you put your hand on my head?"

He told me that the Holy Spirit was flowing into me and that he was just the person God used. Then John asked me to put out my hands with the palms facing up. He placed his hands about an inch above mine, but he was not touching me. He looked me in the eyes. "Do you feel it?"

I closed my eyes and told him yes. It felt as if my hands were receiving some sort of energy from his hands. It was the same energy I felt when he laid his hand on my head, but he didn't touch me this time. I asked him how he was doing it. He told me that God uses him to transfer the Holy Spirit to others. Then John explained that anyone could do this. "Anyone? Even me?" I asked.

He said, "Yes! Try it."

So I did. He placed his hands palms up in front of me, and I put my hands one inch above his hands. I felt energy come out of my hands and into his. This was the first time I experienced the Holy Spirit going in and out of my body. What happened that evening was proof that what the Scripture talks about and what other Christians profess was real. It was an amazing phenomenon. As you can imagine, this specific evening changed my life and the way I look at my belief in God.

So no, I am not just my body. My body believes in God, but my spirit is able to receive Him. That is a big difference. This truth will impact your life forever. I couldn't wait to tell Jerry about my experience with John the next day. I woke up at about five o'clock the next morning and saw John on his knees, praying in front of his bed on the other side of our room. His bed was in front of the window, and the sun was rising. Such comfort filled the room. I couldn't sleep anymore, so I stayed in bed, closed my eyes, and prayed as well. At breakfast, I shared my story with Jerry. All he did was smile at me in a way that 1 will never forget. His expression said, "I know how it feels, and I'm glad you get to experience it as well."

The next stop was Bucaramanga, a small town with an airport located north of Bogotá but east of Medellin. We visited an orphanage where young kids ranged between six and sixteen years old. All these kids were happy, and joy filled their eyes. This eye-opening experience opened my mind and view of life because I thought the kids had nothing. But they had everything they needed: a roof over their heads, someone who cared for them and loved them, a school where they could learn, and most importantly, healthy food to eat. In fact, we ate lunch with them and had a great meal. We stayed in Columbia a few more days, and I got the opportunity to meet several more spiritual leaders and attend more services.

I was blown away by how people lived in South America, how happy they were, and how fulfilled they were with fewer material possessions. The pastors and spiritual leaders had a wonderful way of looking at life and added so much value to the people in their community. I will never forget my Bogotá experience.

"Therefore, if anyone is in Christ, the new creation has come. The old has gone, the new is here!"
(2 Corinthians 5:17).

I am convinced that whether sooner or later, every one of us will have a Bogotá experience at some point in our lives. Once it happens to you, it will change your life, and you will never be the same.

ABOVE AND BEYOND
Even after numerous failures and disappointments, you must go above and beyond your limitations. This is what will keep you alive and help you stay positive. You can experience an inner push to become a better person than you were yesterday.

Choose to take one new baby step in the right direction. Let go of the sadness holding you back from being available to your present life.

POSITIVE AFFIRMATION AND VISUALIZATION
As I have previously said, your book of life was already written before you were born. The day you were born, your

life was already provisioned. When God saw you for the first time at birth, he was so proud of you. He was proud because he made you perfect—perfect for Him. In God's eyes, you are beautiful and talented.

"Be perfect, therefore, as your heavenly Father is perfect" (Matthew 5:48).

Many, if not all of us, try to figure out what we want to be and do in life. How many times have you asked kids or teenagers what they want to be when they grow up? Usually, the answer is, "I'm not sure yet. I don't know. I have no idea," or something similar. God has already predetermined what He wants you to do on earth, and He has already given you provision to accomplish it. All you need to do now is open that book and read the first chapter of your story. You may ask yourself, *Well, how do I do that? Where do I start?* I am a firm believer that your parents are responsible for showing you how to open your book in life.

If your parents showed you strong values and principles as you grew up, you probably had a pretty good idea of which direction to head. They guided you, which is important.

> *God has already predetermined what He wants you to do on earth, and He has already given you provision to accomplish it.*

Parents don't need to tell their children what to do, but they should guide them. Guidance pushes you gently in a certain direction in life: school, a professional career, a job, or church ministry. Why do you think preacher's kids tend to follow the parents' footsteps within the church? Why does the child of a pilot typically lean toward aviation? Why do children of doctors usually end up working in the medical field? It is because they have received guidance and been influenced by their parents.

A parent is a role model. If we don't have that guidance provided to us or if we feel lost in life and don't know what we need to do, a Christian will start praying. You can then visualize what you would like to be. I call it influencing your subconscious mind and feeding it with the power of the Holy Spirit. I will explain how this works for me. For three weeks, every morning when I woke up and every night before bed, I prayed and ask for specific things. I believed so much that I would get what I wanted that it became a habit for me.

See, our subconscious mind is stupid; it is the part of the brain with reasoning and cannot tell what is real. Just think about the last nightmare or dream you had. When you suddenly woke up, your heart rate was increased, and you were sweating. When you were dreaming, this process took place subconsciously in your mind. When you wake up from a nightmare or dream, you realize that no one is chasing you. That's because your conscious mind identifies you in your bed, in your bedroom, safe and sound. Your conscious mind is smart and can differentiate between reality and fiction. Your subconscious mind cannot.

Another example is habits. Habits come from repetitive actions: doing the same things over and over. The habit may make you feel good or cause you to feel bad. Either way, consciously, you feel comfortable doing it. A routine is hard to break. For example, I drink coffee every morning, but if I skip a day, I feel as if something is missing in the morning. I have tried substituting coffee with tea or water, but it's simply not the same. The fact is that after three weeks, you can create a habit by doing something every day.

One day, I decided to stop eating meat. I saw a documentary about athletes who lived on a 100 percent plant-based diet. The result was more energy, higher stamina, weight loss, increased strength, less tiredness, and better health. Even their blood work showed improved health. It is proven, and I saw it. After I watched the documentary, I stopped eating meat and changed my diet the very next day—not the next week, the next month, or sometime in the future. I gave myself a deadline, and the deadline was the next day.

I could not wait to improve my health. Changing my diet had nothing to do with the environment, animal rights, or emissions. It was only about me. It is important to know that I was the biggest meat eater in the house. I ate the biggest steaks and the greasiest bacon slices every day. Sometimes I had meat at breakfast, lunch, and dinner. I was so convinced and had such a strong feeling about improving my health that I had no problem changing my diet. A few days went by when I didn't eat meat. Then a week, then a month, then six months, then a year. As of the writing of this book, I haven't eaten meat regularly for over two years.

The Centers for Disease Control data shows the incidence of obesity among adults aged twenty years and older increased by 30 percent over approximately fifteen years. In 2015–2016, the prevalence of overweight or obese adult men was 75 percent and 68 percent for women.[8] When I read these numbers, I did not want to be one of those statistics. When I changed my diet, I was heavy but not overweight, but I knew I was not healthy.

A year later, after doing more research, I also decided to give up dairy products: milk, eggs, yogurt, and cheese. Oh, my goodness, was that weird. I loved cheese and eggs and ate them every day. I gave it all up. I was determined that this would change my life for the better, and it did! I lost weight, I feel more energized, I'm not tired during the day anymore, and all in all, I feel fantastic. I have good news for you: If I can give up eating the foods I once loved—meat, meat products, cheese, and cheese products—then you can too!

If you consciously do something every day for three weeks straight—and I'm talking about every day, not just Monday, Tuesday, Wednesday, and Fridays, no, every day!—you will be surprised that your subconscious mind has been re-programmed to a new norm. Remember, your subconscious mind is stupid and does not know any better. You train your subconscious to do something for a certain amount of time, and then your subconscious will believe that the new habit, whatever it is, is normal. Now, this may be positive or negative. Yes, you can influence your subconscious

---

[8] "Adult Obesity Facts," CDC.

positively or negatively because there are bad habits, just like there are good ones.

If you keep visualizing what you want and pray every morning, every night, and even during the day, it is amazing what you can attract. Some people call this the law of attraction, but I call it the law of answered prayers. I am a believer, a Christian, so I believe that God does what He wants in my life. There's a difference between a believer and a nonbeliever, between an obedient Christian or just a regular Christian. I'm going to put it in black and white here. Some call them hypocrites, and I call them regular Christians.

When you leave a church service, how often have you been cut off or beeped at in the church parking lot by the same people who were just sitting next to you in the pew? They were worshiping with you, praying with you, and listening to the same message the pastor was preaching. Here's the difference: true Christians live out what the pastor preaches from the Bible. True Christians live like God. What does that mean? It means that you do what God wants you to do. For me, it is serving others before serving myself. I put others first; that doesn't always benefit me personally to start with, but in the end, I am rewarded tenfold.

You must also be ready. What I mean is that you should only ask for something when you are completely ready to receive it. If you are praying for more work, you'd better be ready for it. If you are asking for more money, you'd better be ready to manage that additional money, not just spend it.

What's the point of that? The money I receive is not my money anyway; it's God's money. You don't take any money with you when you die, and your last shirt doesn't have any pockets. You've heard this before many times. Again, if you ask for something, you'd better be ready to receive it because, whatever you ask for from God, He will bless you with infinity. That's a lot.

The next important step is to judge correctly by being ready to receive now. Yes, aren't we all good at that? Sometimes we judge people too quickly, don't we? We don't even know a person but judge them on how they dress, eat, speak, or even what they believe in. You must first be able to judge yourself. Your tongue can curse or bless; you are the judge. Will you speak foul words or humble and kind words? You are the judge.

"Ask and it will be given to you; seek and you will find;
knock and the door will be opened to you"
(Matthew 7:7).

When you start intentionally serving others, God will start moving in your life. Like a thermostat in my house, I have learned to place a demand on what I want. Do you want to set it at 78°F? You determine what temperature to set the thermostat; then the heater kicks on. Do you want it cooler? Then set it to 68°F, and the air conditioning will turn on. "Ask and you shall receive" is the same principle. And guess what? It works! Don't give up.

Learn to solve problems, deal with issues, fight for them, and strengthen vulnerable areas. Get out of your poverty mentality. How often do we say to ourselves, *Oh, I don't deserve that. This is not for me. It is way too expensive. It's out of my league. I will never have this.* For example, when you go grocery shopping, you might compare prices on certain items, such as fresh fruit. Do you tend to buy the cheaper of the two products and look at the price rather than the quality? I agree that sometimes price doesn't justify quality, but my point is that we tend to look at and compare products and choose the less expensive ones. We'd rather buy the purified water than the fresh spring water, which is more expensive. We'd rather buy the cheaper, processed, packaged sandwich meat than the deli meat for a few cents more.

I look at the body like a high-end car: If you drive a Ferrari, you don't put the cheapest gasoline in the tank. If you drive a Porsche, you don't put the midgrade gas in your tank. No, of course not! You put the most expensive, high-grade fuel in your favorite car. When you own your car, you take care of it. When you rent a car, you only drive it and don't pay for cleaning or maintenance. How many times have you returned a rental car after you washed, vacuumed, polished, waxed, emptied the trash out, and filled up the tires with the proper tire pressure? I certainly have never done that.

We rent a car rather than own it. We should own—not rent—our bodies. Our body is precious, and we only have one. The body is self-healing, but that doesn't mean we shouldn't start taking good care of it. Start eating healthy. Put expensive, high-quality food in your body and have an ownership mentality. Judge what's good and bad for you. Decide if you want to live a long, healthy life or a short, unhealthy life. Typically, people change their eating habits and eat well after they get sick or something bad happens to their bodies or if a doctor tells them to change their diet.

Many people would rather take prescription drugs than cure the root cause of their sickness. Often, medical doctors have very little education regarding nutrition. It is like when a person goes through a bad stretch in life, and they experience difficulties. They may ask, "Why is this happening to me? Why do I live from paycheck to paycheck? Why do I have family problems? Why don't my friends like me? Why am I facing so many challenges at work?" Rather than looking at the root cause, people make excuses and often blame others rather than seeing their part in it. We really should go back to the root and see what God wanted us to do in the first place. If we focus on Him first and do what He wants us to do, I guarantee that our lives will be much different than they are right now.

THE HEAD AND NOT THE TAIL

Be the head and not the tail, be the lender and not the borrower. We have a saying about "the tail wagging the dog." This means that something is fundamentally out of balance when an unimportant issue is given far too much weight when making a decision. The tail should not be dictating the dog's direction—the head should do that.

Stop wandering around for years and years, trying to find a path to your future and goals. Start obeying the Lord, and you can expect all the blessings you can imagine. Alternately, you can expect all the curses if you disobey.

"The Lord will open the heavens, the storehouse of his
bounty, to send rain on your land in season and to bless all
the work of your hands. You will lend to many nations
but will borrow from none. The Lord will make you
the head, not the tail. If you pay attention to the commands
of the Lord your God that I give you this day
and carefully follow them, you will always be at the top,
never at the bottom"
(Deuteronomy 28:12–13).

The head is the leader who decides and charts the course while the tail must follow along. The head decides where to go and what to do while the tail has no say in the matter.

FOLLOW JOY

Many of us do what's expected of us. We get up, get ready for work, and commute, sometimes for an hour or more each way to a job that we dislike. In most cases, it's just a job that pays the bills, but we have no passion or inner fire for our work. Our workday consists of tasks that we don't particularly enjoy, and at the end of the day, our work doesn't bring us any satisfaction or joy. We tend to live for the weekends, which are spent doing fun and exciting things if we're lucky. But they often become just another workday because of all the chores at home that have piled up during the week. We push down the unhappiness and emptiness by buying stuff, but in reality, those things don't make us any happier. Instead, they just put us into debt, which ties us down even more to that job we don't like.

So it's a vicious cycle that we need to escape. Unfortunately, it is very easy to become used to this lifestyle. We become comfortable and complacent and stop living passionately and purposefully. Interestingly, we are feeding this energy to people who are unhappy and unfulfilled. Think about the attitude of unhappy people; they don't care. They don't care about their bodies, and they don't care about their place in life. On the other hand, happiness creates an upward spiral of compassion and caring. So what does that have to do with learning how to follow your joy? Everything! Joy is a practice and not just an experience that you fall into.

Here are three steps for you to take each day:

BE YOURSELF

Many of us fear not being accepted if we are real. We have been taught to compare ourselves with others the majority of our lives. This started when we went to school and continued from there. So it's normal to fear being different. Discover your true joy by simply becoming more aware of what moves you and makes you happy. Try to focus on the joy of just being you, the you that you remember before you began to believe it wasn't cool to be you. Remember, your book was written the day you were born; we need to open the cover and start reading our chapters, not rewrite our pre-destined purpose.

When we were kids, people would tell us, "You can be whatever you want to be." Well, guess what? Now is the time to believe in yourself again and do what brings you joy and happiness.

DON'T WORRY ABOUT WHAT OTHERS THINK OF YOU

I know this is easier said than done, but you can and should practice this if you want to live the life you feel you deserve. The rest of the world is far more concerned with what they believe people are thinking about them anyway. Fill your cup with joy first; then you can choose to share with others later. Pray about how right it feels for you when you do follow your own joy. People around you might not get it, and they might not support you either. But always remember, it's not your job to please others, especially if it's at your own expense. Some may say this is selfish, but in this instance, do it anyway. Your life and happiness can rub off on others and inspire them to live authentically. If they don't elect to do so, it is not your job to fix them because that's their own choice and not yours.

DO IT FOR YOURSELF

You must be patient; there's a difference between escaping from your life and consciously choosing to enjoy the present moment as it comes. The present moment is the only reality, so do more of what you love right now and don't worry about the future. Do it now, not tomorrow. You will feel what happens when you focus on the joy of the moment. Be thankful and thank others. Think about what's in the moment that brings a smile to your face. What makes you feel grateful? What can you do today that makes you feel good? Remember, don't wait to do things your way. Your joy doesn't need to pay the bills; it just needs to be part of your life, purpose, and chapter in your book. Do what you love, be joyful, be yourself, and live in the moment without guilt or fear.

"But as for you, be strong and don't give up, for your work will be rewarded"
(2 Chronicles 15:7).

I want you to live your dream. You don't have to ask for it—it comes to you! By dreaming through faith, you will attract your future. You will become attractive, and your future will come to you. If you are obedient to what you are supposed to do, you will receive the needed support and assistance. In your spirit, you must accept that God values you. He has all these wonderful plans for you. We need to stop criticizing and build each other up. Encourage yourself and others to live their dream. Never give up. I know it's really up to you, and it's not the time to give up.

6 | CLEARED FOR TAKEOFF

Be brave. Take risks. Nothing can substitute experience.
—Paulo Coelho

Vision without action is merely your dream.
Action without vision just passes your time.
Vision with action will change your world.
—Joel Barker

Visionaries look into the future and see things not through the lens of current reality, but through the lens of future possibility.
—Kara Claypool

VISION

The first time I experienced having a vision was when I was an intern with Qantas Airways, the airline where my mom worked. I was sixteen years old, and it changed my life; as a teenager, I knew what I wanted to become. My mom arranged for me to work with a flight engineer on a Boeing 747–200 airplane. On "bring your kids to work day," I went to work with this flight engineer for one week, flying back-and-forth between Frankfurt, Germany, and Amsterdam, Netherlands. Although it was just a one-hour flight each

141

way, I spent twelve hours with my mentor, whose name was Ian. He was the maintenance manager for the Frankfurt and Amsterdam stations. The airplane came in full of passengers from Sydney, Australia. Some passengers were dropped off in Frankfurt and then continued to Amsterdam.

I had the opportunity to join the flight in Frankfurt, and I was given the jump seat in the cockpit to observe the flight engineer, copilot, and captain for the entire flight. As a sixteen-year-old, that was a big deal. Although I had been on many flights before this, I had never had the opportunity to witness the whole process with the procedures for takeoff, cruise, and landing. I accompanied Ian each step of the way as he completed the pre-flight inspections on the ground for the Boeing 747. I flew in the cockpit as an observer and then accompanied him to the backstage operations at the airport where no passengers were allowed to go. I saw background activity I had never seen before, and I was so amazed that I began envisioning myself in the cockpit of the 747 one day. I never quite made it to the 747s, but I became a flight engineer on a Boeing 727 and copilot on the Boeing 737 while working with United Airlines.

I felt so important when Ian took me behind the stage and brought me through security with a temporary ID badge in Amsterdam and Frankfurt. I was so eager to become a flight engineer, mechanic, or perhaps even a pilot one day. The experience over this one week changed my mind and created a vision. I had no idea how to execute my vision and no plan of how to become involved in the aviation industry. My mom suggested that I apply for a mechanic apprentice position at Lufthansa airlines in Frankfurt after high school. When you graduate from high school in Germany, you can either continue to university or attend a trade school and technical school. I decided on the latter because I was always practical.

So in 1990, I began as a mechanic at Lufthansa. In the first year, you learn to work with aluminum, steel, and polycarbonate materials. You learn how to rivet, how to use a drill bit, a lathe and milling machine, and work on sheet metal—all the basics of being a machinist. In the second year, you go to the different departments of the maintenance shop of a big airline. I went to the power plant shop where they overhaul and repair airplane engines and then to the brake shop where they disassemble airplane brakes from 737s, 747s, and Airbus airplanes. Additionally, I went to the instrument department where the calibration of instruments and tools took place. The third year was the most exciting because we worked on the airplane itself.

I was part of a team conducting big A, B, and C checks. Every year, the airplane undergoes certain routine maintenance, including completely taking apart the interior, cleaning components, exchanging pumps, changing filters, and updating avionics. A ten-year maintenance check of an airplane takes about two months to complete. We also completed daily routine checks that are conducted between the time when the airplane lands and takes off again. The daily check includes tire pressure, oil level, the general condition of the airplane, and fluid and oxygen levels.

When I was sixteen, I envisioned myself doing something that I wanted to do. I imagined it repeatedly. I was persistent in finding out how to reach a certain position in the industry, and I looked for people who could connect me with and recommend me to the right people. All these are part of the key to getting where you want to be.

I have thought of the concepts of vision and the future my entire life. I have always been a daydreamer. I didn't always understand how to execute my dreams, but I discovered goal setting when I was an intern.

I began writing down my goals for becoming a pilot. I was determined. I accomplished my goals and became a commercial pilot. I was so excited and proud of myself for that huge accomplishment. Twenty-seven years later, I have achieved many more goals. I knew that I wanted to share my story with you but never quite knew how to start. I had a vision and was determined but had no execution plan on how to write a book. How would I begin?

As I shared earlier, it was not until I was in the car with my friends Kevin and Kathi when, out of the blue, Kathi said, "Sven, you should write a book." I looked at her and explained that I had always wanted to write one and had thought about it for the past ten years.

Kevin, who has written more than fifty books—yes, fifty!— in less than five years, turned around in the front seat and said, "I'll help you get started." I had no plan for ten years until I was gently pushed over the edge to begin writing one word at a time. It is amazing how a spark ignited a dream. *My dream*. What would ignite your dream? How can you be gently pushed?

This book is intended to spark and ignite your dream for your desire and vision. Whatever it is, I hope I can inspire you to take the first step toward the finish line of your vision. In my case, I began writing the very next day. I was so excited and determined, which propelled me to write down the titles of each chapter that I wanted in my first book. I had so much on my mind that I knew I wanted to share with you that I was writing hours each day after that. The draft grew and took shape as I went along. I was so motivated to add value to you, to share my story, and to tell you that it is not hard to make a difference in your life and in the lives of others.

I started by creating a physical and virtual workspace that is with me everywhere I go. I just sit down and type on my computer. If you would like to have this too, make sure to place writing materials in your space: a writing pad, pens, pencils, and sharpeners. Make sure you eliminate all distractions. I either sit comfortably in my chair or walk around and gather thoughts into ideas. I pray and meditate. I ask for help. Be sure to have a plan. Why do you need a plan? Because a plan will bring focus, clarity, and boundaries. Here is the importance of those three items:

FOCUS
The overall direction you want your life to go.

CLARITY
The specific road you want to take.

BOUNDARIES

The parameters you set for decision-making. If you know what you stand for, you can apply the principles to problem-solving.

Now, ask yourself these three questions and commit to answering them honestly. Respond in the way that is most comfortable for you. You can take time with your answers or write down the first thoughts that you have.

1) Who am I?

_____

_____

_____

_____

2) Who am I becoming?

_____

_____

_____

_____

3) What is my purpose?

_____

_____

_____

_____

One tool that I use is making my own "mind clips." I do this by closing my eyes and envisioning what my future could look like. Then I play the movie in my mind. For instance, I can see myself signing autographs for my Amazon bestselling book and adding value to as many people as possible.

VISION STATEMENT

Reflect on your answers to the above questions and the movie you created in your mind. Write out your own vision statement. My vision statement is "To encourage and inspire others to live fulfilled lives and raise everyone's awareness of their personal gifts." Start by filling in the space below. You may need to revise it several times before it is complete. It is important to note that your vision statement will remain the same; it should not change as you move toward it.

MY VISION STATEMENT:

_____

_____

_____

_____

_____

_____

NOTE: Make a personal commitment to complete this section before moving on.

MISSION STATEMENT

Your mission statement is the path you take to reach your vision. It is fluid, and unlike our vision that remains the same, it *can* change. You can have more than one mission statement. So far, I have two—one for my writing and one for my business. You may want to create a business mission statement and a personal one. It is yours, and you have the power to create it. Now take your vision a step farther by answering these questions to guide your mission statement.

1) **Who do you want to add value to?**

_____

_____

_____

_____

2) **Why do you want to add value?**

_____

_____

_____

_____

3) **How do you want to add value?**

_____

_____

_____

_____

Once you have answered these questions, you can use them to form your mission statement. A vision is something we live *to*. A mission is something we live *from*. I hope you feel the momentum!

GOALS

We are now ready for one of the last sections: goals. A goal must be clear and specify how to achieve your mission statement. Your goals must also have time limits with a time frame to accomplish it. This is very important. You are only limited by your own creativity and imagination. Each mission statement should have more than one goal.

Example: My goal is to begin writing my second book by January 1, 2022.

Now it is your turn. Come up with at least one goal (with a deadline) that brings you one step closer to your mission statement.

My goal is to . . .

_____

_____

_____

_____

TASKS

Finally, you must have specific tasks to help you achieve your goals; you take your ideas and put them into action steps. Fill in the blanks. This is your plan. Go for it!

Example: Task 1: I will develop the chapter titles for my second book. Task 2: I will write at least two paragraphs of my first chapter.

_____

_____

_____

_____

"Now faith is confidence in what we hope for and
assurance about what we do not see"
(Hebrews 11:1).

7 | WALK THE TALK

It's not about "what can I accomplish?" but "what do I want to accomplish?" Paradigm shift
—Brené Brown

I learned that courage was not the absence of fear, but the triumph over it. The brave man is not he who does not feel afraid, but he would conquer that fear.
—Nelson Mandela

Courage is what it takes to stand up and speak, courage is also what it takes to sit down and listen.
—Winston Churchill

To unlock your potential, you must walk the talk, which means you put your words into action. It is a version of the everyday phrase "practice what you preach." This is essential to your success. Here are the five steps to unlock your potential. Are you ready?

1) **Vision**
2) **Intentionality**
3) **Courage**
4) **Humility**
5) **Service**

151

VISION

When I first was introduced to airplanes, I fell in love with those big round aluminum tubes with attached wings and powerful engines underneath. I even fell more in love with airplanes when I saw what you could do with them. You can fix them and, of course, fly them. When my mom suggested that I apply as an apprentice with Lufthansa at the age of eighteen, I had a clear vision of being a pilot one day, working on those airplanes as a mechanic. I didn't start out as a pilot right away; no, I started working on them as a maintenance apprentice. I learned the basics of maintenance, read the manuals, got my fingers dirty, and connected with people.

I knew I wanted to become a pilot when I saw the pilot training facility, a building where all the pilots trained to qualify in a specific type of aircraft. The building was full of simulators for many of the various airplane manufacturers. I became friends with some of the trainers, and they showed me how to become a pilot. I had to take a three-day pilot test. The airlines hired pilots off the street and paid for all the initial pilot training back then. It was still a lot of work, and you had to pass the three days of torture. I went to the testing facility; seventy other applicants were there on the first day. We had to pass several written exams with testing on English, math problems, and memorization. You can prepare for these tests in many places, but I did not have the money to do so. Other applicants had an advantage because they had taken prep courses and knew what to expect.

When we had finished, we were called back into a separate room. The seventy applicants were reduced to thirty who had passed. On the second day, they tested our cognitive and motor skills, and they tested how well we could multitask complex problems. We were asked to do certain maneuvers in a flight simulator. This flight simulator is not even close to how professional pilots train; it is a small monitor with a joystick and throttle on the table. All they wanted to see was whether we could operate the joystick in maneuvers. It's not rocket science as it's kind of like a flight simulator on your home computer. While completing these maneuvers, they gave us math questions that we had to type in on a keyboard next to us. After the math questions, a series of four lights flashed: green, red, yellow, and blue. You had to push the button within two seconds. Oh wait, do one more math question while climbing to a different altitude; now there's a green light, hurry and push a button. We're descending, now take a left turn at a certain airspeed. You get the idea.

After that day of training, I thought I had washed out. We were given a certain standard for each successful task. I had high hopes, and in my mind, I was so determined to become a pilot that I believed in myself, believed I had passed this test. Of the thirty applicants, only eight made it to day three. Training captains and human resources held a panel interview on the final day. They asked many questions about scenario-based situations and how I would handle them. It was a typical airline interview that included human resources. Later that same afternoon, they told me that I had passed the three-day interview process. They congratulated me and told me that I had a guaranteed job after passing the two-year Lufthansa pilot school. This included training in Phoenix, Arizona, then going back to Germany to finish up flight training in simulators and line training in the actual aircraft.

You can imagine how excited I was, and I could not wait to tell my family and friends. It was too good to be true, right? But there was a catch. In the past, Lufthansa paid for all your training if you passed the three days of training. However, they had changed the policy, and now the pilot-in-training was responsible for all training costs—about ninety thousand German marks (roughly fifty thousand dollars back then). If you did not have the money, you would have to take out a loan with the bank.

They gave me a list of four different banks to contact and negotiate terms with. Now, you can imagine how scared I was taking out a loan in that amount without any guarantee that I could maintain my medical certificate, which is a requirement to keep my pilot certificate up to date. Just imagine if I didn't qualify for a medical certificate two years into my flying career. I would still owe all that money to the bank with no guaranteed way of repaying it. I did not feel comfortable borrowing that amount. Instead, I declined the offer for the guaranteed job with the airline. If I had accepted, perhaps I would be celebrating more than thirty years of flying transcontinental, international flights in the biggest jetliners you can imagine.

I went back to complete my mechanic apprenticeship, and while I was doing that, I worked as a part-time realtor with a friend of mine and sold a few houses. I saved that money along with the money I earned from selling my car and some of my electronics, a total of fifteen thousand dollars. I researched and found a book called *Flying in the USA* that explained how to get your pilot's license in the US and then convert it to a European license. I was so intrigued by the author on how much easier, quicker, and especially cheaper it was to get your pilot's license in the US.

I graduated as an airplane mechanic on June 16. On June 17, I was on a US Air airplane headed to Saint Augustine, Florida, where I selected a private flight school to attend with many European student pilots. The very next day, on June 18, I had my first student pilot lesson in a Cessna 152. Three weeks later, I had my private pilot certificate in my pocket. Yes, only three weeks later! I flew an average of six hours a day, studied four hours a day for the written exam, and passed my private pilot check ride. I continued my instrument, commercial, multi-engine rating and took my first flight as a student pilot within ten weeks. I had to take three written tests and complete several flight stage checks and my final check ride with the FAA. I had a vision, which was very clear in my mind. If I can do it, you can do it too.

INTENTIONALITY

When you are intentional, you choose to make decisions and act based on what is important to you—being intentional means getting clear about what you want to achieve up front. You intentionally set out to accomplish a specific outcome or result in the future that is important to you. When I started flying as a student pilot, I was so intentional that the air

155

sickness I had at the beginning of my flying career gradually decreased. Yes, I was airsick. You may wonder, *How can pilots get airsick?* Well, go and fly for the first time in a small two-seater airplane through turbulence in the afternoon when it is 90°F. Of course, not everyone gets airsick, but I did. I overcame it intentionally by focusing on my goal—the goal of becoming a professional pilot.

So what does it mean to be intentional? The first step is knowing what you want. By identifying your values, dreams, priorities, and goals, you can do that. Why do you get out of bed each morning? What is your purpose, and what makes you feel alive? Once you have answered those questions, the next step is to align your actions accordingly. How do you spend your time, money, and energy? Are you living in alignment with what matters most to you? If not, what needs to change? This doesn't mean that an intentional life is perfect, but it's purposeful. It's finding the courage to let go of what no longer serves you and pursuing what makes you feel alive.

You will still make sacrifices and trade-offs, but you know what you're giving up and why when you live with intention. I gave up a guaranteed job with a major German airline where I could fly the biggest equipment and most modern fleet. I intentionally followed my values. For me, it was more about the journey rather than the task itself. No matter where you are in life, you know that the choices you make and take every day will ultimately bring you a sense of purpose and satisfaction.

Here are eight ways to be intentional every day:

1) Be aware of the media you read and watch.
2) Choose to be kind.
3) Do what brings you joy.
4) Prioritize what's important.
5) Practice good listening skills.
6) Ask "why" before you buy.
7) Make time for self-reflection and prayers.
8) Know when it's time to let go.

"In all this you greatly rejoice, though now for a little while you may have had to suffer grief in all kinds of trials" (1 Peter 1:6).

You can be intentional by doing something that brings you joy. It is powerful for adding value to your life, but it's often overlooked. Unfortunately, I think that's because we've been conditioned to put the hustle before our happiness. We usually feel as if we need to be productive all the time, and we feel productive when we're working toward this acceptable definition of success. But what is that? What is your definition of success? Is it about getting the most done every day, or is it whatever makes you happy? The point is, find even just a few moments every day to do something that brings you joy and

> **" You can be intentional by doing something that brings you joy. It is powerful for adding value to your life. "**

completely changes how you feel about your life. Be sure you are intentional about making yourself a priority.

Most people work and trade time for money. This means that if you earn fifteen dollars an hour and buy a fifteen-dollar sweater, then you have sacrificed an hour of your life in exchange for an item of clothing. The real question is, are you properly compensated for your talents and gifts at work? Or are you just working for a paycheck? How does that make you feel? Before buying something, ask why and question how and even if that item will add value to your life. Then ask yourself if it is worth being paid for your time or your gifts and talents.

Setting aside time for self-reflection and prayer is essential for intentional living; it shows you if you are on the right track. Simply take a few minutes every day and reflect on your values and priorities. Then ask yourself about your schedule. Anytime you're not happy with your answer, you should work on aligning yourself. When a car pulls to the left or the right, it's time to bring it to the shop and get it aligned. And you are the same: Your life can't be pulling you to the left or to the right. You must have a clear path, straight ahead without anyone pulling you to the left or to the right. Finish up by setting your intentions for the next day, week, or even month. This will help you stay focused on what matters most to you.

Finally, everyone should be intentional about prioritizing rest and self-care. Take time out of the week and do something for yourself: get your nails done, go for a massage, read a book, swim, or work out. It is vital to take care of yourself. You might be able to get by without self-care for a while, but eventually, you will neglect your physical and mental well-being. If that happens, you will run out of steam.

So many things can weigh us down—physical clutter as well as our own thoughts. We may struggle to focus on what matters because we're too distracted by everything that doesn't. The real solution is to let go. Declutter your closet, clean up your home, let go of the past, and practice self-forgiveness. Try to learn how to let go of the little things that bother you and stop comparing yourself to everyone else. I know it's not easy, but with practice, you can get better at releasing everything that holds you back. And guess what? This creates space for a more intentional life.

COURAGE

When I decided to go to flight school in a city where I didn't know anyone in a country where I had never lived before, I was uncomfortable. When you don't have any friends or family and move to a new location, especially a country with different cultures, it is very lonely. You don't know if the city is safe or dangerous, if there's violence or not. It takes courage to move. I had to go into a very uncomfortable situation when I was in my twenties. I left my comfort zone and stepped away from what was familiar: my surroundings, my home, my friends, and all my family. I took one bag with me to a place I had never been before where I would stay for an undetermined amount of time.

159

I felt like an outsider. I felt weird speaking a different slang and accent than the people around me in Saint Augustine. The funny part is that the people I hung around with—my flight instructors, neighbors, and the other students—were so intrigued by my accent, my name, and the fact that I was foreign that they begged me to go out with them. They thought I was cool because I was different. I felt accepted and special, and being different became a positive quality, which was new to me. In Germany, I always fit in; I didn't stand out because I wasn't different from anyone else. I went with the flow, and I fit right in. Now in a totally different country, I was completely different from the average person. I stood out, and it was positive. If you are different from others, that's a great advantage. No matter how different you are, you are special.

Courageous people stand up against what threatens them or for what they care about. These people act in a way that is consistent with their values. Sometimes the action does not need to be loud; instead, the action can be quiet and thoughtful. I encourage you to be bold and dedicated, which is part of being courageous. Dedication is a single-minded focus on something you decide on. It is a commitment you make toward achieving a goal. As a result of the dedication, you're willing to sacrifice almost anything in your life. Many of us focus our time, resources, and even our entire lives to what we are dedicated to. Everyone has their own journey to becoming a dedicated person. Not only do

> *Courageous people stand up against what threatens them or for what they care about.*

you express your dedication differently, but you also choose different areas of your life to be dedicated to.

Dedicated people are passionate. Sometimes we think of dedication with a twist of negativity. In some instances, dedication is doing something even if we don't quite like it. So if we want to be dedicated to something and stick to it, we had better be passionate about it. Dedicated people keep their promises. In fact, dedicated people underpromise and overdeliver.

It's about your word. Back in the day, your word meant something; nowadays, not as much. Why is that? Because values and principles have changed. If you are dedicated, you don't shy away from your responsibility. Many of us have a negative view of responsibility. We look at it as a burden we must carry. We often do not want to take responsibility for anything we don't have to. But responsibility is not a burden; in fact, it's a privilege. Dedicated people also know to learn from their mistakes and move forward; they have to own up to what they did wrong and work to ensure that something like that never happens again. That's why dedicated people understand the valuable lesson that mistakes teach us. Instead of playing the blame game and staying stuck in the past, dedicated people reflect on their mistakes and then refocus their goals. Dedicated people are also dreamers and believers. They believe that they can do something that seems impossible to others. Don't you dream? I am a dreamer.

HUMILITY

The Merriam-Webster Dictionary defines humility as "freedom from pride or arrogance."[9] Being humble is the act of humbling yourself. Pride could be a positive trait (feeling good about yourself and your accomplishments), but it can also be negative (viewing yourself as better than others). I believe someone with humility has a *growth* mindset. Humble people recognize that no matter how good they are at something, they can still be and do better. I believe this is what's needed for success. Being humble doesn't mean that you can't be proud of your accomplishments; you can show your humility to people around you in many ways.

When you lose a soccer game, you congratulate the other team and learn from that experience. If you have been wrong or made a mistake, you apologize. The most important thing is that you take responsibility and hold yourself accountable. So many of us don't do this. Bring people up rather than pull them down. Humility is a great self-improvement tool, and without that, you won't be successful. Humility helps us to be more honest with ourselves. You have to be *honest* with yourself. That is so very important! Humility helps you pick yourself back up after you fall.

Here's what I've learned: Humble people are also confident people. It's not all about seeing your weaknesses but understanding your strengths and using the right tools to find success for yourself. Now the question is, how do you build

---

[9] *Merriam-Webster.com Dictionary*, s.v. "humility (*n.*)," accessed March 19, 2022, https://www.merriam-webster.com/dictionary/humility.

confidence? Take a moment at the end of each day and reflect on your accomplishments. You have to celebrate all your small wins because success is an accumulation of all your small wins.

As I look back at what happened to me when I left Germany, I can see that the best things really happen outside your comfort zone. You will never find success if you're busy living within your comfort zone. You have to get comfortable with discomfort. It will increase your chances of success because you'll be more open to taking risks and jumping into the opportunities that will come along during your journey.

I definitely took a huge risk moving to the United States and giving up everything I had in Germany. What will you do? What are your next steps? You must reflect on your behavior because it directly influences your thoughts. Self-reflection shows you whether you are on the right path. By taking time for daily self-reflection, you can correct your behavior and decisions before it gets too late and you get off the path. The bigger the risk you take, the greater the reward. Use a journal for self-reflection. You can review it weekly or every month. For many months, I wrote in my journal every day. Journaling is simple and effective and will increase your happiness. I use *The Five Minute Journal*.

Every morning, I write down at least three things that I am grateful for. You will be amazed at how many things you can be grateful for. Here is an example from one of my days:

- I am grateful for God,
- I am grateful for all His blessings, and
- I am grateful for my health.

It's not so hard, is it? Next, I consider the question, "What would make today great?" and list three things. Here is my example from one day:

- Walking in the park
- A nice dinner with Carlos
- Take ten minutes to read *Rich Dad Poor Dad*

Here's the most important statement you can declare every morning: "I am." This open-ended affirmation will push you past your limitations.

"I A M"

This is a space where you can write anything:

- I am smart
- I am successful
- I believe God will do good things for me
- I attract business, new friends, and wealth.

For example, here is what I affirmed every day for four weeks: I am attracting positivity, happiness, and wealth in increasing amounts from increasing sources.

Guess what happened after just four weeks? Friends were knocking on my door, I had a more positive attitude, and the most amazing thing was that my business was not just growing but exploding. I received calls from clients I had not heard from in months and years, calls from individuals I had never done business with before. I guarantee that you will attract what you ask for. You must be ready for it though.

What is important is that you are specific, especially with your goals. Avoid being general, or you aren't setting a true goal. In other words, instead of saying, "I would like to have a nice dinner with my friend," write down exactly what you want and with whom you want to do it: "I want to have dinner with my cousin Carlos at Houston's."

The last thing I do when I journal is ask myself, "How could I have made today even better?" This question causes me to self-reflect on areas where I missed an opportunity. Self-reflection is incredibly important. Get out of your comfort zone, be direct with yourself, and be honest and persistent. Commit to writing in your journal every evening for at least four weeks.

Focus on the positives and remind yourself of your strengths. Too often, we are told to work on our weaknesses. Everyone has weaknesses, but why would I focus mainly on my weaknesses? Yes, of course, we do have to work on our weaknesses, but we need to focus on our strengths *more* than our weaknesses. Ask yourself what you did well today. How can you continue to improve? Taking pride in your accomplishments doesn't deny the fact that there's always room for growth.

Here are some ways to be live more humbly and my thoughts about them:

ADMIT YOU ARE NOT THE BEST

Accept and admit that you won't be the best as someone will always be better than you. The primary way to learn humility is to admit to yourself that you are not the best at everything even when you try your hardest. You never get a trophy when you come in last.

IDENTIFY YOUR WEAKNESSES

Try to recognize that people come with strengths and weaknesses. The quicker you accept this fact, the more humble you can become. All of us have our own flaws along with the best parts of ourselves, but not everyone accepts them. You must recognize and accept them.

BE GRATEFUL EVERY DAY

There's a big difference between arrogance and gratitude. You need to know when and how to draw the line. Be thankful for all your strengths and what you have achieved. Avoid bragging about your accomplishments, especially when people around you didn't ask you.

ADMIT MAKING MISTAKES

You should never run away from mistakes you have made in the past. Take responsibility because you are ultimately accountable for your own mistakes—nobody else is. When you make a mistake, instead of running away, admit it. Avoid becoming defensive and making excuses.

NEVER BRAG

Here is an unspoken rule about being humble. When people ask about your accomplishments, offer a high-level response. No one wants to be around somebody that brags about their life. Remember, it's about how you say it. Keep parts of your life private rather than putting them out on a posterboard,

VALUE OTHERS

There is something special and pure about humble people when they value others. The ability to identify somebody you really appreciate is a key to humility. Again, words go a long way. Your tone and the way you say those words matter. Walk the talk. Remember that talk is cheap. Do it!

OTHER PEOPLE COME FIRST

Consider other people's feelings. Tone down your accomplishments as not everyone wants to hear about them. If you are already a generous person, you will probably have an easier time with humility since you always put the needs of others above your own.

ALWAYS LISTEN

The most important factor that sets a humble person apart from an arrogant person is that a humble person will go out of their way to listen to what you have to say. Listening and hearing are two different things. Hearing does not necessarily mean that you are processing the information; whereas when you listen, you think about what the person said. There's a big difference. An arrogant person only hears so that they can then talk about themselves. Become a good listener if you want to become more humble.

FEEDBACK IS ESSENTIAL

Whether positive or negative, humble people aren't afraid to receive all kinds of feedback, especially when they know that it can eventually improve their lives. Accept constructive criticism, even when receiving negative feedback, which is not the easiest thing to hear.

Here is the key takeaway about humility. You do not know your own limits, so you have to keep pushing yourself to learn, grow, and develop. As far as you know, there are absolutely no limits to your own abilities, which means there's no limit on what you can do to enrich your life and future.

Serve
To perform duties or services for (another person or organization)[10]

Who do you serve? I serve:

_____

_____

---

[10] *English English Dictionary*, s.v. "serve (*v.*)," Voc App, accessed March 20, 2022, https://vocapp.com/dictionary/en/en/perform+duties+for+another+person+or+organisation.

SERVICE

Serving is one of the most important traits of leadership. It's so interesting that service, humility, courageousness, intentionality, and having a vision are all leadership traits that also unlock your potential. The potential of all the dreams you have within you unlocks the chains of the book that was written about you before you were born so that you can become the *you* that you always wanted to be.

Jesus is our greatest model of leadership. His leadership style was unlike anyone else's. He was a servant leader. In the book of Matthew, Jesus outlined how to be a leader and defined leadership as a humbling act of servanthood. The fastest way to gain leadership is by serving via a problem-solving approach that includes your team in the process.

> "Jesus called them together and said, 'You know that
> the rulers of the Gentiles lord it over them,
> and their high officials exercise authority over them.
> Not so with you. Instead, whoever wants to become
> great among you must be your servant, and whoever wants
> to be first must be your slave—just as the Son of Man did
> not come to be served, but to serve,
> and to give his life as a ransom for many'"
> (Matthew 20:25–28).

Earlier in the book of Matthew, Jesus was met by a great crowd of people, many of whom were diseased or disabled (Matthew 15:29–39). As they were laid at his feet, Jesus healed them. Jesus went a step further in meeting the needs of the people, and he used a problem-solving approach as outlined below.

- He identified the problem and informed his team (v. 32).
- He instructed them to brainstorm the solution (vv. 33–34).
- He invited them into the problem-solving process (vv. 35–36).
- He included them in a solution (vv. 35–38).

Through this act of service, Jesus went on to feed more than four thousand people who had come to him in need of healing.

Servant leaders focus on other people's needs and not on their feelings. Servant leadership is not a leadership style or technique but a lifestyle that you adopt over the long term. As a servant leader, you choose to serve first. You focus on the needs of others, especially your team members, before you consider your own.

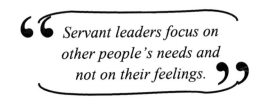
Servant leaders focus on other people's needs and not on their feelings.

Acknowledging other people's perspectives gives them the support they need to meet their work and personal goals. Involve your team in decisions to build a sense of community. This will lead to higher engagement, more trust, and stronger relationships. This applies to the CEO of a company, a sibling, the drummer of a high school marching band, or a volunteer at your church; leaders and leadership opportunities are everywhere.

"To do what is right and just is more acceptable
to the Lord than sacrifice"
(Proverbs 21:3).

So how do you become a servant leader? The most important quality of a servant leader is integrity. God has called us to walk in the ways of righteousness and justice, and our actions as servant leaders should reflect this. We are called to lead with integrity, which includes not cheating, lying, or being manipulative. Instead, we must lead differently than the world does. We lead by being honest.

Jesus consistently tells us to humble ourselves and live our lives with integrity. Today's society tells us to do whatever it takes to achieve success. In school, our youth are taught to dress and act a certain way to be noticed. It will require intentionality to lead with integrity. You may fall short; after all, you are human. When true servant leaders stumble, they confess their sins before God and those they lead. It's always better to confess when you mess up instead of covering it up. Living life with integrity, especially with challenges and temptations, is an incredible way to be a witness of God's goodness to those who look up to us. How many times have you been told, "Wow, that was very brave and humble of you to do?" Whatever it is, whatever it was, you've likely been there before. Doing a good deed goes a long way, especially if nobody's watching—that is true integrity.

"Therefore, as God's chosen people, holy and dearly loved,
close yourselves with compassion, kindness, humility,
gentleness, and patience"
(Colossians 3:12).

It can be difficult to admit that we don't know it all. A servant leader can learn and grow from the experiences and opinions of those who are wiser, more knowledgeable, and more experienced. We must be willing to learn from and listen to those we lead because we know that they have value and worth. In many cases, you will find that the people you lead have better ideas than you do or, at the very least, a different perspective. Learning from others will expand your view of God and His creation.

"I am not saying this because I am in need, for I have
learned to be content whatever the circumstances. I know
what it is to be in need, and I know what it is to have
plenty. I have learned the secret of being content in any and
every situation, whether well fed or hungry,
whether living in plenty or in want."
(Philippians 4:12–13).

In this verse, Paul maintained a positive attitude even on his worst days. He teaches us that just like circumstances, attitude can change. Attitude can be improved if we learn the secret. And attitudes have a source for their strength.

STEWARDSHIP

God has given so many different spiritual gifts to His people. Can you just imagine what life would be like if everyone thought, looked, and acted the same? Yes, boring! When you hear the word "stewardship," your mind may go straight to the topic of money, but there is more to stewardship.

"Each of you should use whatever gift you have received to serve others, as faithful stewards of God's grace and its various forms"
(1 Peter 4:10).

According to the above verse, every one of us has at least one spiritual gift. The spiritual gifts we receive from God are intended to serve people, not boost our reputations. Spiritual gifts are meant to be stewarded by us; we are not the owner—God is.

God definitely wants us to be good stewards of our belongings and our finances; however, this is not the only thing we should steward. We also need to be good stewards of all the people God has placed in our lives—all of them, not only a few. We need to see people as valuable to God and steward their time and talents well. We should call out what is good and true about the people we lead. We ought to mentor, coach, and encourage them as well. How much does it cost to praise an employee at work? Positive words would be a breath of fresh air out of our mouths. Praise goes a long way; you give, and you get back tenfold.

The spiritual meaning of the number seven is perfection, so here are my seven rules for unlocking your unlimited potential:

SMILE
It always works out in the end to have a smile on your face.

BE KIND
Make people feel good; they will make you feel good.

NEVER GIVE UP
Find alternatives when the first time doesn't work out.

DO NOT COMPARE
Everyone is different, which is good; we would not all want to be the same.

PROMOTE POSITIVITY
Think and live positive thoughts, which promotes a healthy and successful life.

MAKE PEACE WITH YOUR PAST
Focus on the present and create your future; you can never change the past and what happened.

TAKE CARE OF YOURSELF
Eat nutritious food and meditate through prayers.

"Therefore encourage one another and build each other up"
(1 Thessalonians 5:11).